# THE ECONOMICS
# OF NATIONAL ISSUES

ROGER LEROY MILLER
University of Washington
and
National Economic Research Associates

RABURN M. WILLIAMS
University of Hawaii

# The Economics of National Issues

Canfield Press, San Francisco
A Department of Harper & Row, Publishers, Inc.
New York / Evanston / San Francisco / London

THE ECONOMICS
OF NATIONAL ISSUES

Inflation, unemployment, wage and price controls, income taxes, the public debt, interest rates, the balance of payments—these broad national issues are of perpetual interest to laymen and professional economists alike. During periods of our history when the nation is faced with seemingly grave policy dilemmas, these issues take on special significance.

The past few years have been such a period, with the United States experiencing levels of inflation and unemployment that have visibly shaken both the public and the politicians. Torrents of economic verbiage inundate us in the press and on television. Suddenly the heretofore "dismal science" finds itself on the covers of *Life* and *Newsweek*. Yet being in the spotlight somehow doesn't seem to have clarified the issues for anyone, let alone the experts. Economic policy making these days is often befuddled and confused, and the classic solutions are declared no longer relevant. At times it is disturbing to realize that courses of action taken by men in high places affect the economic life of every one of us. In spite of this, there seems to be little consideration of the fundamentals essential to an understanding of macroeconomic problems. In this book, we attempt to give the careful reader sufficient background so that he, at least, may be able to distinguish the rhetoric from the real issue when confronted with current debates about national economic policies.

For those students who have had no training in price theory, we suggest that the second, third, and fourth chapters be skimmed or skipped altogether, at least during a first reading. We suggest that the chapters be read in order, with the possible exception of those mentioned above.

When economic concepts are first introduced, we have tried, with some consistency, to italicize them. Many times we have inserted the more technical terminology in parentheses.

This book is meant to be a supplement to existing and future principles textbooks. We also feel it will be a useful companion to textbooks on public finance, monetary theory, international trade, and money and banking. All graphical analyses and references are given in the *Instructor's Manual*.

Several people helped us in the preparation of the manuscript. Our colleagues Peter Frost, John Allen Hynes, and James Jonish made extensive comments on an earlier manuscript, for which we are thankful. Jon Cushman helped with gathering historical information. We especially wish to thank Judith Ann Williams for the time she spent helping with the revisions. Susan Vita Miller also made comments on the final manuscript. All remaining errors are solely our responsibility.

Roger LeRoy Miller, Seattle
Raburn M. Williams, Honolulu
August, 1971

# CONTENTS

# THE ECONOMICS
# OF NATIONAL ISSUES

# 1
# THE ECONOMICS
# OF THE SHRINKING DOLLAR

The constant increase in the cost of living in the United States is a phenomenon which none of us has been able to avoid noticing. Rising prices now seem as inevitable as death and taxes. We are continually reminded by newspaper and magazine articles that today's dollar is only worth 30 percent of 1939's dollar. Although prices haven't always gone up at our current rate—5 to 6 percent a year—they have been rising at a compounded rate of almost 1 percent a year from 1867 to the 1960s. The pace of inflation, however, has not been even. Some episodes in our history presented us with much higher rates, and some, much lower, even to the extent of causing falling prices.

The greenback period was one episode in our inflationary history that demonstrates how bad things can get. After the start of the Civil War the Union government found itself hard pressed for funds. There wasn't an income tax until 1862, so all revenue came from public land sales, certain excise taxes, and import duties. Once the war was under way, import revenues fell to almost nothing. The Civil War cost money (as wars have a tendency to do). In order to finance the war effort, our government saw fit to issue large quantities of *fiat* currency, called officially U.S. notes, but unofficially nicknamed greenbacks because they were printed in green. By 1863 there were almost $450 million of them floating around—fully one-half of the total circulating currency.

The U.S. Treasury did not back greenbacks with hard metal—gold or silver. Rather it was a *fiduciary standard*, which meant people had to trust the government to make good the paper dollars it was issuing. As more and more of these paper bills were issued, the price of goods in terms of greenbacks rose rapidly. In fact businessmen started quoting two prices: a gold price and a greenback price.

During the entire greenback episode the cost of living in terms of paper dollars fluctuated. After having shot up at 25 percent a year during and after the Civil War, the price index *fell* at the rate of 5.4 percent from 1867 to 1879. That is equivalent to a halving of the price level in less than 15 years. Farmers and businessmen during those years of falling prices cried out for higher prices—inflation and "greenbackism," as it was later called.

When prices continued to fall after an initial upsurge in the early eighties, the new cry was for free coinage of silver in the hope that prices would rise. Politicians apparently didn't listen too well to those cries, for prices fell on average 1 percent a year from 1879 to 1897.

Historically, rising prices have generally been associated with prosperity, and falling prices with the lack of same. Back during the free silver days when prices were falling, William Jennings Bryan felt that the adoption of a pure gold standard without the monetization of silver would lead to continuing deflation and misery. In his oft-quoted Democratic presidential nomination speech, he demanded, ". . . you shall not crucify mankind on a cross of gold."

As better extraction methods and new gold discoveries in South Africa, Alaska, and Colorado increased the supply of this metal, "cheap" gold became the standard in the U.S., and the cries of the silverites were calmed. Prices rose 2 percent a year from 1897 to the start of World War I.

Prices then rose 16 percent a year from the start of the First World War to a few years after it. They fell drastically for several years after the war and then remained fairly stable until the Great Depression. Wholesale prices dropped at an average rate of 8 percent a year from the Crash until 1933, when Franklin D. Roosevelt declared a "banking holiday" in March of that year. Roosevelt's attempts to raise prices were successful, and there was general inflation until 1937. Then prices leveled off until the beginning of the "greatest war in history."

The rate of price rise during the Second World War was less than during both the Civil and First World Wars. The wholesale price index rose 118 percent from August 1939 through August 1948.

From 1948 until the mid-sixties prices remained quite stable except for a jump during the Korean War. Since Vietnam, inflation has accelerated. Perhaps by the publication of this book prices will be rising at somewhat less than the current 6 percent, but we won't bet any money on it.

The U.S. is not alone in its history of continuing rising prices. Inflation seems to be a worldwide problem. In fact our rate of inflation is mild relative to many. Other countries have had periods of hyperinflation which make our wartime episodes look like ripples in the monetary ocean. In 1939 Hungary had a price index set at 100. By January 1946 it was almost 5,500,000. One-half of a year later it was 20,000,000,000,000 or $2 \times 10^{13}$! Inflation of 20 percent to 100 percent a year, and more, is common in many Latin American countries. While prices in the U.S. have risen about 30 percent since 1963, they've risen just as much in Italy and more in France. Japan can boast a 50 percent increase in the same period.

Misery may love company but numerous international bedfellows will not alter the effects of inflation. The question is, do we necessarily suffer because of inflation and, if so, is the suffering "equitably" distributed?

Although we have generally observed a correlation between deflation and misery, inflation certainly does not always mean prosperity, and even if it did, not everyone would benefit. When prices rise *unexpectedly*, all those who have given credit to others are repaid in "cheaper" dollars. The purchasing power of a dollar falls as the price level rises. Any obligation fixed in terms of (nominal) dollars will cause creditors to lose and debtors to gain when the price level goes up before account can be taken of its rise. The moral, of course, might be to borrow all you can if you think there is going to be an inflation and nobody else does.

If, however, everyone anticipates rising prices, the cost of borrowing (interest rate) will go up. Creditors will demand higher interest rates to compensate for the depreciated purchasing power of the dollars repaid. Debtors, anticipating this decreased purchasing power of the dollars to be repaid, will willingly pay the higher interest rate. For example, if you know that prices will rise 5 percent by the end of next year, you won't lend money unless you are compensated for the loss in purchasing power of the dollars to be repaid you. That is, you will charge 5 percent more than if you had expected no inflation. So instead of, say, 3 percent or 4 percent interest, you'll demand 8 percent or 9 percent.

All of us are in some sense bondholders because we carry cash—dollar bills—around. A dollar bill is basically a non-interest-bearing bond from the government. Its expiration date is infinity and it pays zero cents a year interest. Anyone holding cash during an inflation loses part of his *real* as opposed to *nominal* wealth when prices rise. The real value of your cash is what it can be traded for, what it can buy. When the price level goes up, the same amount of cash no longer buys as much. If you kept an average checking balance of $100 in 1971, its purchasing power would have fallen by about 6 percent by the end of the year. Inflation therefore causes people to lose purchasing power in proportion to the amount of cash they generally keep handy. The only way to avoid this loss of purchasing power is to keep no cash balances. But life without cash can be very inconvenient. Notice we are referring to cash, not income. We use cash because it facilitates our daily transactions. Imagine having to make *all* your purchases only on the days you received your paycheck or scholarship.

Because currency and checking accounts are useful in making our life easier, we say that cash allows for more productive use of time. You don't have to resort to barter to get what you want with your income. You don't have to worry about putting all of your income in interest bearing investments every day because of the prohibitive cost of keeping cash. Businesses don't have to employ larger numbers of money managers to extract every last cent of interest on any unused income.

Inflation also has the effect of raising the average income tax rates because of our progressive income tax system. In the U.S., as you earn more (nominal) income, you enter successively higher marginal tax brackets. Since the tax schedule does not shift very often, rising nominal income due to inflation puts more and more people in higher and higher tax brackets. That means that even with no growth, the government will collect a larger and larger share of national income. When inflation pushes everyone into higher tax brackets, the productivity of the country is also affected because the payoff for working falls relative to that for not working. Leisure becomes less "expensive" as the income tax gets larger.

In addition to the specific groups of people who can be hurt by inflation—creditors, bondholders, and those with cash balances—historically, people with fixed incomes have suffered. Other people, believe it or not, have benefited. We shall look at who gained and who lost during the inflationary sixties. The first part of the decade saw price stability, the second part, price increases starting at 1.3 percent a year up to the current 6 percent a year.

Looking at the aged, who are generally reliant on fixed incomes, the period 1964-68 saw their real standard of living fall. Social security did rise as much and more than the price level, but the payoff from other retirement plans, bonds, and fixed dollar value financial assets such as savings and loan shares did not. It actually fell.

Historically, all those who have income which is fixed in nominal terms will lose with an unexpected inflation. If, on the other hand, people are certain that prices will rise in the future, they will demand retirement plans which offer increases in nominal income so as to maintain at least a constant real standard of living during their retirement years.

Union workers also lost out during the latter part of the sixties. Union workers are usually covered by longer-term contracts than nonunion workers. Hence even though prices started to rise, many unions had to wait to get wage increases. For the 3-year period 1967-69, union wage rates after taxes hardly rose at all in terms of purchasing power. Since then, unions have attempted not only to make up for lost growth in real wages but to build into their contracts their expectations of a continuing 5 to 6 percent inflation.

Andrew Brimmer of the Federal Reserve found out that the distribution of income changed in the direction of more equality during the period of high economic activity in the later sixties.

Ultimately, no general statement can be made about being better or worse off during inflation. Individually, we must look not only at our wages but also at the value of all our assets. We must compare any changes in nominal quantities with changes in the purchasing power of the dollar in order to arrive at an idea of the real, as opposed to nominal, increase in our income and assets. It appears that real wages did not rise in the latter part of the sixties, so many workers did not improve their lot. But we can easily discover why this happened: no one expected prices to rise as rapidly as they did. If everyone is sure that prices will keep on rising at their current rate, workers will demand contracts which include purchasing power adjustments every year; bondholders will demand a yield (interest rate) which includes an inflationary adjustment; and retirement plan purchasers will demand variable, inflation-adjusted future incomes. The only people who cannot completely avoid all negative effects of long-term, correctly anticipated inflation are those who hold cash—that is, all of us. We have to pay the inflationary tax on the use of currency and checking account balances so long as we choose to use them.

We could always ask the government to stop taxing our cash balances and to increase our other taxes, but it does not necessarily follow that this would make us any better off, as we shall see in the following chapters.

# 2
# THE ECONOMICS
# OF A TAXPAYERS' REVOLT

After several years of living with the threat of a taxpayers' revolt, after 13 days of Senate debate during which 111 amendments were prepared, after strong opposition from President Nixon against closing off several glaring tax loopholes, the Tax Reform Act of 1969 was finally put into law. The list of reforms is indeed impressive; the act

1. Increased deductions from $600 to $750 over a 3-year period.
2. Increased social security benefits by 15 percent.
3. Extended surcharge (down to 5 percent from 10 percent) for another 6 months.
4. Repealed 7 percent investment tax credit for machinery and equipment, retroactive from April 19, 1969.
5. Postponed reductions in excise taxes on telephone services and new auto purchases.
6. Reduced gas and oil depletion allowances from 27.5 percent to 22 percent.
7. Lowered taxes for single people to ensure no more than 20 percent higher taxes for singles than for married people.

8. Increased from 10 percent with a $1,000 ceiling to 15 percent with a $2,000 ceiling the standard deduction for nonitemized returns.
9. Provided minimum standard deductions of $1,100 designed to relieve 5.5 million low-income taxpayers from paying taxes.
10. Provided a minimum 10 percent tax on most kinds of "tax preference" (tax-free) income in excess of $30,000 (a taxpayer could continue to get tax-free treatment on an amount of excess income equal to his normal tax liabilities).
11. Placed a $50,000 ceiling on the amount of individual capital gains eligible for the alternative, or lower, tax rate of 25 percent.
12. Raised to 32.5 percent for 1971 and 35 percent for 1972 the maximum capital gains tax for individuals on their excess above $50,000.
13. Gained a 4 percent audit tax on investment income of private foundations and provided restrictions on attempts by private foundations to influence legislation and elections.

The declared net result of this change in our tax structure is a $2.5 billion decrease in revenues for the government. The expected net tax reduction phased in over a period of years amounts to $8 billion a year at projected 1975 income levels.

While the name of the game was obviously reform, many observers thought otherwise. After returns were filed in 1971 for calendar 1970, the *Wall Street Journal* found that the Tax Reform Act of 1969 "left many spacious (tax) shelters untouched." It was noted, however, that it was now harder for highest-income individuals to pay zero taxes.

The debate about the effectiveness of reform and about which taxes should be raised and which lowered is bound to go on until either government ceases to exist or until resources become free. In the meantime, we can examine at least some historical and theoretical aspects of different types of taxation.

The Constitution gave Congress the authority "to lay and collect Taxes, Duties, Imports and Excises. . . ." No specific reference to an income tax was made then, but the Wilson-Gorman Tariff Act of 1894 provided for individual income taxes of 2 percent on incomes above $4,000. (It also allowed for taxation of corporate income, which we discuss below.) Even though the country knew about income taxes from paying $5.5 million of them during the Civil War, the concept was violently challenged and finally had to be settled by the Supreme Court in 1895. With the passage of the Sixteenth Amendment in 1913, no more court ruling was necessary. Section II of the Underwood-Simmons Tariff Act of that year provided for a 1 percent rate on taxable income with an exemption of $3,000 plus $1,000 more to a married head of household. A surtax was levied progressively on income over $20,000, with a maximum total tax rate of 7 percent on income over $500,000. While these rates seem paltry compared to today's, they were considered large in those times. Also, the concept of *progressiveness* was first introduced then, and met with considerable debate.

Today there is widespread belief that the rich should pay more. This belief does not, however, constitute a complete case for progression. Progressiveness causes the rich to pay *progressively* more. As an individual earns more income, he is subject to higher and higher marginal tax rates, while all previous rates are left unchanged. A progressive schedule such as is in effect today has rates, for joint returns, ranging from 14 percent on the first $1,000 of taxable income up to 70 percent on anything over $200,000. The *average* tax rate, therefore, never reaches the *marginal* rate. In 1961 for example, when the top bracket was 91 percent, the average rate paid by those in that bracket was less than 45 percent.

There have been three theories used to justify this type of progressiveness: *ability-to-pay*, *benefits*, and *sacrifice*. The ability-to-pay concept assumes that high-income earners can afford to pay more than low-income earners. But justification of this doctrine must further specify that ability to pay goes up *more than in proportion* to income. A similar addendum must be added to the benefits doctrine in order to justify progression: benefits of the high-income earner must increase *more than in proportion* to income.

The sacrifice theory of taxation hypothesizes that since rich people are sacrificing less by paying taxes because they have more than the poor, they should pay higher taxes. This argument assumes a very special relationship between extra (marginal) income and the utility derived from it. To justify progressive taxation, the sacrifice theory must rely on the supposition that the (marginal) utility of income for the rich is less than for the poor.[1] While this supposition is intuitively appealing, especially to those of us without high income, it's really a proposition which would be difficult to prove.

The progressive nature of our income tax has had, at least theoretically, some effect on general productivity. When wages are taxed, the price, or opportunity cost, of *not* working falls. This is true not only with a progressive tax, but with any kind of income tax. An income tax, therefore, other things being equal, induces people to work less, that is, to buy more leisure. This is called the *pure substitution effect* of a price change. But of course other things do change. An income tax reduces spendable income for the individual. The tax imposes an *income effect* on him. There is an incentive to work more, *ceteris paribus*, to make up for this loss in income. What we observe after the imposition or increase of an income tax levied on wages is the net result of both income and substitution effects. Which one dominates depends on the individual's tastes and income. It is hypothesized, for example, that the income effect is stronger the closer an individual is to the "subsistence" level of living. We note, for example, that when relatively large wages were paid poor natives in Algeria, their American employers found that few returned to work after 1 or 2 weeks of wages. The income effect overwhelmed the substitution effect. Historically in the U.S., the income effect has dominated. As real

[1]Formally called diminishing marginal utility of income.

wages rose at an annual rate of 1 percent, there was a reduction of 0.25 percent a year in hours worked during the period 1900-57. Part of this reduction, though, is due to the progressive nature of the income tax, as mentioned before.

As people earn more nominal income, they find that the cost of *not* working goes down because their marginal tax rate goes up. For an equivalent tax revenue obtained, people will always work less in the face of a progressive tax as opposed to a proportional one. (Proportional taxation taxes all income at the same rate.)

Professor A. C. Harberger estimated that work effort would have been 2.5 percent higher for lower-income-bracket people and over 11 percent higher for higher-income people in the absence of the progressive tax system. People have succeeded in reducing work effort by voluntary absenteeism, going into their own businesses with their own hours, taking longer vacations, retiring earlier, and moonlighting less.

This reduction in work effort may be even more pronounced if the U.S. continues to experience the current high rate of inflation. Although the marginal rate for the upper brackets has been reduced from 91 percent to 70 percent in the last decade, that of the lower brackets has not. Hence, lower- and middle-income earners are being pushed into higher marginal brackets by the effects of inflation on their nominal income. Leisure is, therefore, becoming relatively cheaper.

If progression causes such distortions, is there an alternative? A proportionate income tax would reduce the *increasing* distortion in the labor-leisure choice as income rises, but it would still exist to some extent. Proportional taxation would continue to distort the opportunity cost of not working relative to working.

In place of an income tax, we could have a *general sales tax*. If it were truly general, with the same rate applied to all goods and services bought, it would be analytically equivalent to a proportional income tax. It would be very difficult to transform a general sales tax into anything like a progressive income tax because people don't make all of their purchases at once. The taxing authority couldn't enforce progressiveness.

Finally, we could enact an *expenditure*, or *consumption*, *tax*. People would be taxed on what they spent, not what they earned. Individuals would report their income for the year and their year-end savings. The difference would be taxable spending. A consumption tax could be made highly progressive, even more so than an income tax whose limit is a marginal rate less than 100 percent. A consumption tax would not distort the choice between consuming today and consuming in the future as an income tax does.

Today people are taxed on income even from savings. We save in order to have more income in the future, in order to be able to consume more in the future. How much more depends on the rate of interest we get on our savings *after* taxes. The income tax lowers the after-tax rate of return, increasing the present price of future consumption. With a consumption tax, the cost of consuming in the future is not affected relative to today's prices; that is the price of future goods remains lower by the full amount of the yield on savings.

Whatever the theoretical points about progression, empirically we do not have as much progressiveness as the study of our tax schedule seems to indicate. When account is taken of tax-exempt income and capital gains—the difference between the buying and selling price of assets such as common stocks —actual tax receipts as a proportion of income (including capital gains) fall slightly as income increases. In 1968 people with gross income over $100,000 but less than $1 million payed a little more than 28 percent in taxes; those with incomes exceeding $1 million paid only 25 percent.

Individuals are not the only U.S. taxpayers. There also exists a corporate income tax. Back in 1909 it amounted to a mere 1 percent of total taxable corporate profits (income = total revenues − total costs) and there was a $5,000 exemption. This exemption disappeared by 1932 when the rate had reached 13.75 percent. 1936 saw the first graduated tax schedule similar in form to the current one. Since 1950, corporations have had to pay a normal tax on the first $25,000 of profits, then a surtax on any amount above that. The normal tax has ranged from 30 percent to 22 percent, which is the current rate. The surtax here ranged from 19 percent to 26.67 percent, with the current rate being 26 percent.

Over 95 percent of corporate income is subject to the surtax, that is, a total rate of 48 percent (normal rate of 22 percent + surtax of 26 percent). However, when corporations' long-term capital gains are taken into account, the actual corporate average tax rate is closer to 38 percent. (Remember, capital gains are taxed at less than the regular rates.)

It is often suggested that the corporate income tax is a general tax on the income from capital. After all, income is generated either by one's labor efforts—these are wages—or by one's capital (savings). The corporation pays out all the returns to labor in the form of wages, salaries, and special stock options to executives. After it has paid all its other bills, the result is profit. But what is this profit? It represents income from capital, since labor has already been paid its income.

Granted, then, that the corporate income tax is a tax on the income from capital. But not all income from capital is generated in the corporate sector of our economy. Fully one-half of capital's income comes out of areas of the non-corporate sector such as housing and farming. The corporate income tax is therefore definitely *not* a general tax on the income from capital. All income from capital in the noncorporate sector is taxed at individuals' marginal tax rates which on average are less than the corporate rate. Moreover, the after-tax profits of the corporation are taxed again when the stockholder pays taxes on his dividends or capital gains.

This differential taxation causes a distortion in our economy. Since investors are only concerned with the after-tax rate of return on their capital, there will be movement of capital until (on the margin) the net, after tax, rate of return is equal in the corporate and noncorporate sectors.[2] Because of the corporate income tax, there is less capital in the corporate sector of the economy than there would be if the income tax on capital were applied everywhere equally. Without a corporate income tax, there would then be a smaller number of split-level 4-bedroom houses. Housing happens to be in the noncorporate sector. Many would view this as the wrong direction in which to go since housing "needs" are so "critical." We are here referring only to the *economic efficiency* aspect of corporate income taxation and not to specific social goals. We refer only to the misallocation of resources due solely to the distorting effect of the corporate income tax on the rates of return to investors in the corporate and noncorporate sectors.

Who pays because of this differential taxing of income from capital? In the short run, when the differential first came into effect (and whenever it broadens), the owners of fixed corporate capital suffered a loss in the market value of their capital because the after-tax stream of income had fallen. In the long run, since the corporate sector is smaller than it would have been in the absence of the distortion, the price of goods produced there is relatively higher. Hence people who prefer goods made in the corporate sector must pay higher prices for those goods because the supply is smaller. Workers who can earn higher wages in the corporate than in the noncorporate sector are also worse off because there is less demand for their labor (at each wage rate) since the corporate sector is smaller than it would otherwise have been.

Income taxation, in no matter what form, will always introduce an economic efficiency distortion. Our current system distorts the labor-leisure choice, the savings choice,

[2]The rates we are referring to should be corrected for risk.

and the corporate-noncorporate allocation of capital. Presentation of these effects does not, however, offer a valid argument for *no* taxes. The role of government in our economy is indeed large and useful. Government must be financed and therefore taxation in some form or another is warranted.

# 3

## THE ECONOMICS
## OF BIG BUSINESS' DEMAND
## FOR MORE TAX WRITE-OFFS

"Nixon's Tax Giveaway," "In Defense of Depreciation," "New Trouble for Tax Write-offs."[1] And so went the debate started by the Nixon administration in 1971. Most readers may ask themselves, "What's it all about?"

The debate centers on the possibilities of liberalizing the rules that businesses are allowed to use when they compute *depreciation* on their plant and equipment. Corporations pay taxes only on net profits—the difference between all revenues and all *allowable* expenses. If General Motors buys a new die press to stamp out Chevy bodies, it is not allowed to deduct the full purchase price of the press before it pays corporate income taxes. It can only deduct as a current expense the depreciation of that machine.[2]

If the machine cost $10 million and it would wear out steadily for 10 years, after which it would be worth nothing, GM could depreciate one-tenth of the purchase price, or $1 million each year.

[1] These quotes are article banners from the *Progressive,* the *Wall Street Journal,* and *Newsweek.*
[2] Sometimes called capital consumption.

Obviously, GM, Ford, U.S. Steel, and all other corporations would be better off if the government allowed them to
write off (depreciate) machines faster than they have been
allowed in the past. The Internal Revenue Service (IRS) has a
set of standard guidelines for figuring the "useful service life"
of machines. Nixon proposed that business be allowed to
reduce these specified periods by 20 percent. In the above
example, GM could depreciate its die press in 8 years instead
of 10. If we still assume that the machine will depreciate
smoothly, its new current tax write-off would be $1.25
million instead of only $1 million. With the current corporate
tax rate at 48 percent, GM would have its taxes reduced by
.48 × $250,000, or $120,000, this year.

By now some readers may be wondering why it matters to
a business what it can deduct for the costs of a machine.
After all, the business can still only deduct a total of 100
percent of the purchase price. The timing of this deduction
is, however, very important. Would GM not be better off if it
could deduct the $10 million today instead of, say, at the
end of 10 years? True, the tax "kickback" is the same—$4.8
million—but $4.8 million in hand is worth more today than it
will be worth 10 years from now. GM could, for example,
invest the $4.8 million and end up with quite a bit more in
10 years. As a general rule, any benefit, such as a tax
deduction, is worth more the sooner it is realized. Any cost,
such as a tax payment, hurts less the farther in the future it is
incurred.

Now you can understand big business' demand for more
tax write-offs in the form of liberalized depreciation rules.

Until the 1930s the IRS allowed each businessman to
determine how he wanted to depreciate his capital equipment. The corporate income tax was only 11 to 12 percent
then, so the benefit of quick depreciation was not as great as
it is now. Then, during the Depression the government wanted to get more money out of corporations, so it set up
specific rules for depreciation.

For maximum economic efficiency, depreciation should

accurately reflect the *true* decline in the market value of the asset in question. In a society with no technological change, no change in tastes, and no inflation, true depreciation would relate only to the *physical* deterioration of equipment. In the real world, though, there are technical advances, people's desires for certain products change, and there are varying rates of inflation.

In a dynamic world such as ours, it is a mistake for either the IRS or a business to look at historical costs. A machine may have cost $1 million 3 years ago. Let's assume it has remained unused in its crate in perfect condition. If there has been an inflation equal to 50 percent in those 3 years, that new machine is worth $1.5 million, not $1 million. On the other hand, if a new discovery makes it worthless, then it is only worth the scrap value. We should always look at *replacement* costs instead of *historical* costs.

In spite of the fact that virtually all assets decrease in value proportionately more during earlier years (think how much a new car falls in resale value the minute it's taken off the lot), *straight line* or equi-proportionate depreciation was the rule prior to World War II. Finally in 1954, several forms of *accelerated depreciation* were incorporated into the tax structure. Business can now use either *double declining balance* or *sum-of-the-years digits* depreciation, in which case more than an equi-proportionate share of the asset's purchase price can be deducted in the first few years of its service life. Except in special circumstances, one of these two forms of accelerated depreciation will be chosen over simple straight line because of the general rule stated above: A benefit is worth more the sooner it is realized. Depreciation tax write-offs are worth more the closer they are clumped in the earlier years of a machine's life.[3]

If accelerated depreciation conforms closely to reality, whenever a firm sells a used asset, the *book value* (purchase price minus all depreciation) will equal the sale or market

[3]The present value of accelerated depreciation is higher than the present value of straight line depreciation.

price. If the market price exceeds the book value, then the depreciation schedule has exceeded the actual decline in the asset's value.

From 1962 to 1969 a special type of extra depreciation was on the IRS books. In an attempt to stimulate new investment President Kennedy instituted a 7 percent investment tax credit. All businesses were allowed to deduct from their tax bill owed the government at the end of each year an amount equal to 7 percent of all newly purchased equipment with service life exceeding 8 years. With a corporate income tax of around 50 percent, the 7 percent investment tax credit was equivalent to about 14 percent additional depreciation. Assets had 114 percent depreciation then, instead of only 100 percent, with the extra 14 percent having come during the year of purchase.

Accelerated depreciation may be viewed as an interest-free loan from the government, whenever the accelerated schedules exceed reality. This loan has to be repaid, however, at some later period during the service life of the asset. The investment tax credit is not an interest-free loan, since the tax savings are never repaid. Both methods of tax savings increase the rate of return on purchasing capital, but to the extent that the benefits are not equally applicable to *all* assets there will be a shifting of resources in the economy.

For example, the investment tax credit did not apply to assets which had service lives of less than 8 years. Hence, there was relatively more investment in longer-lived than shorter-lived capital. The credit did not apply to housing or consumer durables, and as a result there was relatively less investment in housing and consumer durables and relatively more in producer durables.

To the extent that accelerated depreciation does not apply uniformly, there continue to be incentives to "overinvest" in some sectors and "underinvest" in others.

There is little doubt that accelerated depreciation and the investment tax credit can stimulate investment in producer durables by increasing their rate of return. Other forms of investment not eligible for the investment tax credit suffer, however, as people switch investment to those assets which yield the highest rate of return.

At one time or another it has been asserted that the aggregate effect of accelerated depreciation and the investment tax credit can stimulate the entire economy. Indeed, this was why President Kennedy wanted the latter. By increasing the rate of return (after-tax profits) of new investment opportunities, Kennedy hoped to increase the demand for equipment and machinery. The increased spending in this sector was expected to spill over into other sectors of the economy.

# 4
## THE ECONOMICS
## OF TAXING WINE, BEER,
## AND CIGARETTES

If you've ever bothered to notice the sales tax on spirits and tobacco products these days, you must have realized how large a tax can become. Many upright legislators have gone so far as to suggest that excise taxes on such "immoral" items be raised even higher so that income taxes could be lowered. Perhaps all of you nonsinners think that this is a good idea because we all know that at some increase in price those "sinners" won't buy any more alcohol and cigarettes. At that point the sales tax becomes *prohibitive*. Believe it or not, though, high tax rates on alcohol and cigarettes can be justified to some extent by economic welfare analysis, which we shall discuss in a moment. Right now, we want to give a little history of sales taxes.

We find evidence of such taxes in ancient Egypt, China, and India. Rome, under Augustus, had a general sales tax of 1 percent on all items except slaves. They were taxed 2 percent! Spain was successful in imposing its sales tax in the 1300s and brought the idea to Mexico in the early 1500s. France was less successful then, but one need only know a little bit about the French character to understand this problem.

The U.S. has never enacted a *general* sales tax at the federal level. Rather, states have instituted their own sales taxes with widely differing rates. We find that those states that do not have a state income tax usually rely heavily on a sales tax for the revenue necessary to run the government. At various times the U.S. has considered a general sales tax, especially when the Treasury has been faced with large demands for revenue, such as during wartimes. However, there have been and still are federal excise or sales taxes on certain items such as telephone service, cars, and marijuana.[1]

Earlier we stated that the effect of a general sales tax was analytically similar to a proportional income tax. Actually, any specific sales tax on a single commodity has the same effect—the good taxed becomes relatively more expensive. For example, when a tax of 5 percent is put only on beer, the actual cost to the beer drinker will go up. If no other good is similarly taxed, the relative price of beer thus rises. Our beer drinker may choose to buy less beer and more wine, say. He will *substitute* away from the relatively more expensive good to relatively cheaper goods. In addition to this pure substitution effect, his real income will fall if he is a particularly avid beer drinker. If he attempts to continue drinking as much as before the tax, he will have to spend more of his income on beer. He will, therefore, end up with less of all the other things. His real income will have fallen. The income effect of a specific sales tax is directly proportional to the proportion of a consumer's budget the taxed good represents. Obviously a member of the Temperance League would not be directly affected by the tax on beer. Normally, when a person's real income falls he buys less of everything.

Taken together, the price or pure substitution effect and the income effect will cause our beer drinker to buy less beer. How much less he will buy depends on his tastes and income.

[1]Although the marijuana tax is no longer on the books, the IRS is still collecting it from persons convicted of avoiding it in previous years.

A person's responsiveness to price changes is measured by his *price elasticity of demand*. If he has a very *inelastic* demand for beer, the rise in price will not significantly cut down his beer consumption. If he has very *elastic* demand, he will reduce his purchases of beer drastically. We say, therefore, that the change in quantity demanded is directly a function of the elasticity of demand. This fact has important implications for analyzing the economic value of goods and services produced in the economy.

We must first discuss how goods and services are valued in society. Each of us individually expresses the value we place on a good by the price we would be willing to pay for it. This price implicitly reflects the amount of other goods sacrificed in order to purchase the good, for increased expenditures on one good must reduce the income available for spending on anything else. The market price of a good, however, does not reflect its *intrinsic* value. The market price merely registers the value of the (marginal) unit purchased. We usually value an additional unit of the good less if we already have a lot of it. For example suppose you were willing to pay 75¢ for your first bottle of beer. After consuming that bottle, you would be willing to pay 50¢ for a second bottle and only 25¢ for a third bottle. If the market price of beer were 50¢ a bottle, you would consume only two bottles of beer, for the third beer is worth less to you than the other goods you would have to sacrifice to obtain it. The price, then, measures the value of the *last* unit purchased, not the *average* value of all the beer purchased. Since beer costs 50¢ a bottle, the economic value of the two bottles of beer is $1.00. The intrinsic value to you is $1.25, for that would be the price you would willingly pay rather than do without two beers. Since you pay only $1.00, you receive 25¢ of value without paying for it. This benefit is called *consumer surplus*. Consumer surplus arises in this case because producers in a competitive situation where information flows freely must charge *you* the same price for each beer.

Another form of consumer surplus is created because producers must charge *all* customers the same price. A business-man who sells a tube of toothpaste to you at one price cannot usually sell it at a higher price to your neighbor, even if the intrinsic value he gets from that tube is greater than yours. Another businessman would be willing to offer your neighbor the tube at a slightly lower price. Alternatively, you would find it profitable to resell the toothpaste offered to you at the lower price. Generally the price to all buyers of similar products, corrected for transportation costs, is the same. Even though your neighbor might be willing to pay more than you for the tube rather than do without, he would end up paying the same. This is another form of consumer surplus. There is no way this consumer surplus can be taken away in a competitive system because competition equates the price paid by all consumers of the same product.

How much do the resources used in making the toothpaste cost? Resources are limited, so producers must bid resources away from other uses. In a competitive economy resources are allocated between competing uses by producers so that they produce the same economic value (at the margin) in all their uses. Any resources producing less than this general economic value will be bid away by producers who can devote them to uses in which they produce higher economic value. The *social cost* (opportunity cost) of producing one additional tube of toothpaste is equal to the economic value of the other goods those resources could alternatively have produced. The price of resources in a competitive economy will reflect the economic value they could produce in other uses.

Competition will induce producers of toothpaste to ex-pand output until the cost of the resources needed to pro-duce one additional tube of toothpaste is equal to the market price of that good. That market price makes the quantity supplied just equal to the quantity demanded.[2] The customer on the margin is just willing to pay the market price for the

[2] The market price is revealed at the intersection of the supply and demand curves.

tube of toothpaste. At a slightly higher price he would not purchase the tube. The marginal consumer receives no consumer surplus. Toothpaste at the going price is no bargain for him. On the other hand all those people who would pay more rather than go without are receiving consumer surplus—they are getting a bargain.

What happens when a specific sales tax is put on beer or toothpaste? The excise tax increases the private cost of beer to consumers. The market price is now equal to the social cost of producing one additional bottle of beer plus the sales tax. Marginal buyers will switch their expenditures to other goods, reducing the quantity of beer demanded. In a full employment situation the excess resources in the beer industry will eventually end up somewhere else, Although marginal consumers reduce their consumption of beer because they are not willing to pay the higher private cost, beer is still worth more to them than its production costs. If there are no excise taxes on goods in the industries to which the excess beer resources flow, the value to marginal consumers of the increased goods produced by these resources will be less than the value of beer sacrificed because the cost to consumers exceeds the social cost of producing beer.[3]

A specific sales tax, therefore, can reduce the economic value of goods and services produced in the economy. We define this reduction as a *welfare cost*. This welfare cost results from distorted prices that do not reflect the marginal opportunity cost of producing the good. The private cost to consumers (i.e., price) is the marginal resource cost plus the tax. People end up buying "too little" beer and "too much" wine, for example.

What about consumer surplus? It will have fallen in the beer industry because of the rise in price. Some of this loss of consumer surplus—the tax rate times the remaining output—is not a part of the welfare loss because it becomes the tax revenue raised by the government. With additional tax reve-

[3]This assumes that there is no distortion between private and social cost in the industries receiving the overflow beer resources.

nue the government can lower other taxes by an equivalent amount, returning the consumer surplus to society. Consequently, this part of the consumer surplus of beer drinkers is merely transferred to society as a whole, embodying no welfare loss.

The less people respond to an increase in price resulting from a given sales tax, the less will be the welfare cost because fewer resources will be shifted into sectors where their contribution to total economic value (welfare) is less. Taxing beer, whiskey, and tobacco at very high rates may result in a very small welfare loss because the price responsiveness or elasticity of demand is extremely low for those items. People just can't seem to live without them. The same holds for food in general but we would not want to push this argument. Since food represents a larger portion of the poor man's budget than the rich man's, taxation of food represents a regressive tax scheme.

When goods are subsidized (negatively taxed), the effect on welfare cost is analogous to the excise tax example. If prospective house buyers are given a 10 percent subsidy from Uncle Sam they will buy more houses, but to construct those houses, resources must be bid away from other sectors where their contribution to total welfare is more valuable. Consumers switch their expenditures to houses because private costs fall. The subsidy distorts price signals. The private cost of housing is the social cost (opportunity cost) minus the subsidy. Whether the price distortion is up or down, there will be some shifting of resources, some change in people's behavior. There will be a welfare cost associated with the resulting misallocation of resources.

In some circumstances, though, taxes and/or subsidies can contribute to the total economic value of goods produced in the economy if prices are already distorted. Since the price to the consumer equals the production costs plus the sales tax, the economic value of the good exceeds the social cost of production by the amount of the tax. If a new sales tax on some other good causes resources to flow into a sector of the economy which is already taxed, total economic value may increase because the economic value of the increased output in that sector will exceed the production costs.[4]

A general sales tax which taxes all goods at the same rate will not distort prices, except that of leisure. The private cost will reflect the social costs. For instance what is the private cost of a beer in terms of the wine you sacrifice to purchase a bottle of beer? The answer is the price of beer divided by the price of wine. If both goods are taxed at the same rate, that ratio remains unchanged.

We end this chapter with a word of warning. Welfare analysis as outlined above does not account for changes in distribution of income resulting from a sales tax. A sales tax on beer, for instance, increases the tax burden on beer drinkers relative to non-beer drinkers. Welfare analysis does not account for the costs imposed on those resources which must be transferred to other uses. All normative ideas about any resulting or given distribution of income must enter into all evaluations of welfare costs and gains from alternative taxing systems. All cards must be laid on the table before we advocate a change in the tax structure.

[4]This is known as the *theory of the second best*.

# 5
# THE ECONOMICS
# OF MAKING MONEY

We all know that the dollar bills in our wallets are printed by the U.S. government. Many of us assume that the government can buy anything it wants by printing that money. Printing money is not the only way the government pays for its expenditures. It can get the money to pay for goods by taxing or selling bonds. The choice of which method is used determines the money supply. The transactions of the U.S. Treasury and of the Federal Reserve combined—plus actions by commercial banks and your tastes for currency as opposed to checking accounts—jointly determine the money supply. *Ultimately though, the Federal Reserve determines which method of finance is used and hence controls the money supply.*

Most people confuse money with income. People receive income; they don't make money. The only people who make money are counterfeiters and the government printers in Washington, D.C. The money supply (narrowly defined) consists of currency and demand deposits at commercial banks. *Currency* in circulation (the dollar bills in your wallet) is a liability of the federal government (U.S. Treasury and Federal Reserve).[1] *Demand deposits* (checking accounts), on the other hand, are liabilities of commercial banks.

Since these two liabilities are indeed different, it is best to separate them for purposes of discussing the determinants of the money supply as we have defined it. The monetary liabilities of the federal government (Treasury and Federal Reserve) comprise what is known as the *monetary base* or *high-powered money*. These liabilities consist of the dollar bills in your wallet and the reserves your commercial bank holds against its deposit liabilities.

Our banking system is called a fractional reserve system because member banks must hold a minimum amount of readily available reserves against their deposit liabilities. Right now big city banks must keep 17.5 percent of demand deposits in reserves, and country banks must keep 13 percent. These reserves, in the aggregate, consist of dollar bills kept in the vaults of the bank and member bank deposits at the Federal Reserve banks, both of which are liabilities of the federal government. These reserves do not earn any interest for banks; they yield no income. Hence, there is an economic incentive to keep as few reserves as possible, consistent with legal requirements.[2]

Let's see what happens if you decide to hold more of your cash balances in dollar bills and less in demand deposits. You go to your bank and demand currency from your checking account. The bank teller cashes your check and the bank's computer is instructed to reduce your checking account balance. Suppose you keep the money under your mattress now. Your total money balances have not changed; you simply hold more currency and fewer demand deposits. Your actions have, however, started a complicated process that will contract the total money supply in the United States.

Your bank lost reserves when you withdrew your demand

---

[1]Don't be fooled into thinking they are the liability of Providence just because "In God we trust" is inscribed on the back.

[2]Even if there were no legal requirements, banks would still hold some reserves to cover net withdrawals.

deposit. Since it held only fractional reserves against your deposit, your withdrawal reduced actual reserves more than it reduced required or desired reserves. For example, suppose the bank must keep 25¢ of reserves against each dollar of demand deposit liabilities. If you withdraw $1.00 of demand deposits, the bank loses $1.00 of reserves. Its required reserves have only fallen by 25¢, so it has deficient reserves. To increase its reserves the commercial bank can sell interest bearing financial assets to acquire cash. (Alternatively it could call in outstanding loans.) When the financial security is sold, the reserves of the bank go up, but the money balances of the individual who purchased the financial security fall, and no one in the nonbanking public experiences an offsetting increase in his money balances. (Remember, the reserves of commercial banks are not a part of the money supply.) If the transacting individual wrote a check to pay for the financial asset, the bank from which it was drawn will lose reserves too. That bank will have to sell financial assets to increase its reserves, decreasing the money balances of another individual. The process continues causing a contraction of the money supply each time a commercial bank sells financial securities to increase its actual reserves. Reserves of commercial banks increase at the expense of the public's money balances. Consequently, one of the determinants of the money supply is the public's desires regarding the form in which they hold their money balances—currency or demand deposits.

What happens to the money supply if the Federal Reserve prints up some dollar bills and buys a bond from you? Suppose you keep part in cash and deposit the rest. Since the commercial bank holds fractional reserves against your deposit, part of the cash you deposited could be used to purchase an interest bearing financial security. When the cash flows out of the commercial bank in payment for the security, the money supply in the hands of the nonbanking public goes up. If the individual who sells the security deposits some of his increased money balances at another commercial bank, that bank will use some of the deposit to purchase securities. Each time commercial banks buy securities with their reserves, the money supply goes up again. Thus, an increase in the monetary base usually causes a multiple expansion of the money supply.

How much it expands, or alternatively, how big the *money supply multiplier*[3] is, depends on:

1. The form in which you and everyone else in the (non-bank) public desire to hold your cash balances.
2. The reserve ratio the commercial banks desire to hold against their demand and time deposits.

If, for example, the money supply multiplier turns out to be 3, $1 of new bills put into circulation by the Federal Reserve will cause a $3 increase in cash balances outstanding. If the Federal Reserve takes $1 out of circulation, the money

[3]One simple algebraic model of the determinants of the money supply relates the money supply (M) to the stock of high-powered money (H):

$$M = \frac{M}{H} \cdot H \tag{1}$$

$\frac{M}{H}$ is known as the money supply multiplier

The money supply is equal to demand deposits (D) plus currency (C):

$$M = C + D \tag{2}$$

The stock of high-powered money may be used as currency in the hands of the nonbanking public (C) or as reserves of the commercial banking system (R):

$$H = C + R \tag{3}$$

Since these reserves are held against demand and time deposit liabilities,

$$R = r_d D + r_t T \tag{4}$$

where $r_d$ and $r_t$ are respectively the reserve ratios held against demand and time deposit liabilities. These equations can be used to derive the following identity:

$$M = \frac{M}{H} \cdot H = \frac{C+D}{C+R} \cdot H = \frac{1 + \frac{C}{D}}{\frac{C}{D} + r_d + r_t\left(\frac{T}{D}\right)} \cdot H \tag{5}$$

supply will contract by $3, after all adjustments have taken place.

Members of the nonbanking private sector can induce changes in the money supply by changing the form in which they hold their cash and time (savings) deposit balances. Commercial banks can induce changes by altering their *desired* reserve/deposit ratios held against their time and demand deposit liabilities. For example, in 1907 and 1929-33 the fear that widespread bankruptcy in the commercial banking system would prevent commercial banks from paying off their deposit liabilities caused a rise in the currency/checking account ratio and in desired commercial bank reserve ratios. The resulting fall in the money supply multiplier contributed to a violent contraction of the money supply. Since the Federal Deposit Insurance Corporation was legislated in 1933, this source of instability in the money supply multiplier has been eliminated. Now most changes in the money supply are due to changes in the stock of high-powered money (liabilities of the federal government) or reserve requirements.

*Both of these variables are under the control of the U.S. Federal Reserve System.* It controls the stock of high-powered money directly through its transactions in the bond market, known as *open market operations*. The members of the Federal Reserve Open Market Committee are, therefore, the most important decision makers in our monetary system. This group consists of the seven Governors of the Federal Reserve System and five out of the twelve regional Federal Reserve bank presidents who are voting members, with the remaining seven presidents being nonvoting members. The committee meets about once a month to issue directives to the Open Market Desk of the Federal Reserve Bank of New York. These directives are followed in its open market operations to achieve some target rate of growth in the money supply or maintain some level of market interest rates. Each time the Federal Reserve buys government bonds from individuals in the private sector it injects high-powered money into the economy, creating a multiple expansion of the money supply.

The Federal Reserve System can also increase the stock of high-powered money by loaning reserves to commercial banks. Federal Reserve banks do not have direct control over this source of high-powered money since they only have the option of granting or refusing loans requested by member banks. Consequently, the open market operations of the Federal Reserve constitute what is the most important method of monetary control because it is the most direct. The demand for loans by the commercial banks can be controlled to some extent by changing the interest charge (the *rediscount rate*). The demand for loans, of course, depends not only on the interest charge but also on the interest yield on financial securities that the borrowed funds may be used to acquire. If the market rates of interest were substantially higher than the rediscount rate, commercial banks would demand large quantities of loans from the Federal Reserve. Consequently, the rediscount rate must move in harmony with fluctuations in the market rates of interest in order to prevent large shifts in the demand for loans by commercial banks. Any change in aggregate loans to commercial banks, however, always can be offset by open market operations.

The net change in the monetary base over any period of time depends on the *net* transactions between the government sector (U.S. Treasury and the Federal Reserve System) and the private sector. Each time the government sector purchases a good or an asset from the private sector, the monetary liabilities (high-powered money) of the government increase. Each time an individual makes a payment to the U.S. Treasury (tax payments, for instance), the stock of high-powered money falls. The Federal Reserve can, however, offset this fall in the monetary base by buying bonds in its open market operations.

The net change in the monetary base of high-powered money is determined by the following accounting identity:

Change in monetary base = Government spending
                                   − tax receipts from the private
                                         sector
                                   − *net* sale of bonds to the private
                                         sector by *both* the Treasury
                                         and the Federal Reserve

If Congress spends $200 billion and the Treasury collects only $100 billion in taxes, the difference must be made up. Whatever fraction of the difference between expenditures and receipts is not made up by net sales of bonds to the private sector must be made up by an increase in the monetary base, that is, by non-interest-bearing liabilities of the U.S. government in the form of dollar bills and member bank reserves.

The government accounting identity requires government expenditures to be financed by taxing in the private sector, borrowing from the private sector (selling financial securities to the private sector), or increasing the stock of high-powered money. To derive changes in the stock of high-powered money, one must subtract the net sale of financial securities to the private sector by the Treasury and the Federal Reserve from the government budget deficit (expenditures on goods and services minus tax receipts). Ultimately, the Federal Reserve determines whether the budget deficit is financed by the net sale of bonds to the private sector or by increases in the stock of high-powered money. The Open Market Committee determines the quantity of government securities to be purchased or sold in open market operations. By changing the discount rate, the Federal Reserve can also change the demand for loans by commercial banks. The resulting changes in outstanding Federal Reserve credit to the private sector can offset any credit flows between the private sector and the U.S. Treasury. *Consequently, Congress and the President determine the size of the budget deficit through their appropriations and taxation decisions; and the Federal Reserve determines how that budget deficit is financed—by borrowing from the private sector or by increasing the stock of high-powered money.*

# 6

# THE ECONOMICS
# OF MONEY AND GNP

Ever since the nomination of Dr. Arthur Burns for Chairman of the Board of Governors of the Federal Reserve System, the newspapers have closely followed his handling of monetary policy. In the beginning of his 14-year term in 1970 the financial press praised his monetary policy. The money supply was evenly expanding at about 5 percent per year. However, as unemployment continued to rise it was suggested that Dr. Burns should accelerate the growth in the money supply. He apparently listened, for the money supply increased at a 10 to 12 percent a year rate during the first half of 1971. The financial press then complained that this was dangerously inflationary.

Anyone reading all these commentaries on monetary policy, as expressed in terms of the rate of growth of the money supply, could get some notion of the relation between it and the state of the economy, but usually only a vague one. Actually, the relationship between the money supply and total spending is one of the oldest ideas in economics.

People hold cash because it facilitates transactions. The services (or convenience) yielded by a stock of cash balances depends upon its *real* value, or its purchasing power over goods and services. People usually desire to hold a fairly constant proportion of their real wealth in *real money balances* (expressed in terms of their purchasing power over goods and services).[1] Empirically, this relationship between the demand for real money balances and the level of real income has been very stable over time. Of course, the demand for real money balances should also depend on the cost of holding them. Since money earns no interest, market rates of interest measure the implicit cost of holding cash balances. John Maynard Keynes is primarily responsible for pointing out the importance of this determinant of the demand for money. However, for analytic simplicity we shall postpone inclusion of the interest rate in our analysis until Chapter 16.

Even if you don't have much control over the total money supply, you can of course determine your own money balances. If your demand for cash balances is less than your supply, you have the option of spending more than you receive. If you'd like to have more cash on hand, on average, you have the option of spending less than you receive. However, with any given stock of money in the nation, what you spend ends up in somebody else's pocket. Therefore, individually we can each determine the level of our nominal cash balances, but together we *cannot* determine the total level of cash balances—only the monetary authorities can do that. Collectively, the public *must* hold the money supply provided by the monetary system composed of the Federal Reserve and the commercial banks (unless people literally burn it up).

The monetary authorities determine the stock of money created by the Federal Reserve System and the commercial banks; the public's actions, on the other hand, create a level of total spending that induces the public to hold that stock of money. Suppose, for example, that the actual stock of

[1]For illustrative purposes, we could assume that $M^d/p = ky$ or $M^d = kyp$, where $M^d$ = nominal money demanded, $p$ = price level, $y$ = real income, and $k$ = constant.

money created by the Federal Reserve and the commercial banks is greater than the public's desired money stock. Individuals will desire to reduce their actual money balances. Each individual can reduce his actual money balances by spending more than he receives. Collectively, however, the public must hold the money stock provided by the Federal Reserve and the commercial banks. If all of us, together, attempt to reduce our money balances by spending more than we receive, desired expenditures will exceed receipts, creating excess demand for goods and services. Output must equal income, for receipts from the sale of output become the income of individuals in the economy. Consequently, if desired expenditures on goods and services are to equal output, desired expenditures must also equal income. If individuals attempt to spend more than they receive, desired expenditures will exceed income (or output). This aggregate excess demand (the gap between desired expenditures and output) will cause a rise in prices and/or an increase in output, both of which will induce individuals to hold larger money balances. Nominal income—output valued at current prices—will stabilize at a level at which the demand for money equals the supply of money.

In a full-employment situation, a sudden decrease in the demand for money relative to nominal income can only lead to an increase in prices or, equivalently, an increase in nominal income. Since in our simplified model the demand for money is some function of income, people will eventually be happy with the existing level of cash balances when their nominal income increases enough. That is, after a while they will stop attempting to get rid of cash balances.

If one follows through with the logic of the above simple model, then, by changing the rate at which the money supply is expanding, the Federal Reserve can alter the rate of growth in total spending (*nominal* GNP). The comments about Arthur Burns's monetary policy refer to judgements about how fast the monetary authorities should induce nominal GNP to increase. Notice that although the rate of monetary growth may be a determinant of growth in nominal GNP, the demand-for-money relationship does not tell us the breakdown of growth in nominal GNP into output and prices. Total spending can go up either through inflation or through growth in output. The breakdown of GNP into output and prices is crucial to stabilization problems. It is that breakdown we shall turn to in the next chapter.

# 7

# THE ECONOMICS
# OF MORE GOODS
# VS. HIGHER PRICES

Today we have rising prices and unemployment. During the first half of the sixties we had falling unemployment rates, very little inflation, and substantial yearly gains in output. President John Kennedy wanted to "get this country moving again," for in 1960 we were in a recession. Less than a year later the country's real output did start moving. From 1961 to 1964, output increased at 5.3 percent a year, from 1964 to 1966 at 6.4 percent. Prices during this first period rose at only 1.3 percent a year, in the second period at 2.5 percent. Then prices took off, first at 4.6 percent a year from 1967 to 1969, then at over 6.2 percent a year for a time during 1970. While prices were skyrocketing, real output was slowing down. From the fourth quarter of 1966 to the second quarter of 1967, output increased at an annual rate of less than 1 percent. Things improved for about 4 quarters to 5 percent a year, but then slowed again to 2.9 percent a year and, finally, from the latter part of 1969 until 1971, output actually *fell* at the rate of 1.1 percent a year.

How can we account for such erratic behavior in prices and output? Why did output and not prices rise in one period, and then prices and not output in the other? While no one has come up with a guaranteed explanation, we can get some idea of the underlying process if we understand what determines *aggregate supply* and *aggregate demand* in an economy. The interaction of these two economic relations determines aggregate output and the price level.

Any supply relationship involves different quantities of output that entrepreneurs will provide at various prices. We shall lump all products and services together here for analytic simplicity, and then we'll be talking about output-price *level* combinations.

As a useful device to analyze supply, we'll assume that producers attempt to maximize profits. Each producer will desire to expand output as long as the cost of producing one additional unit of output is less than the additional revenue generated by the sale of the increased output. In the short run, plant and equipment cannot be increased; additional output can be generated only by expanding the employed labor force (or working the existing labor force overtime). As employment of labor increases, output increases, but at a decreasing rate. The *marginal product of labor* (the increase in output generated by a marginal increase in the employed labor force) decreases because the larger labor force uses a fixed quantity of machines. Each worker has less capital to work with.

For additional simplicity let's assume no producer's output decisions can affect the market price of his product—he is a *price-taker*. In our simplified world, profits will equal the total revenue received minus total costs. When a producer hires additional workers, the increase in profit equals the price of output times the additional output minus the wages of the new workers. Any producer would want to hire more workers as long as that increase in profits is positive. He wouldn't go on increasing employment and output forever, though, even if prices remain constant, for the output each new set of workers adds to the total is diminishing, since they are all sharing the same limited plant and equipment. Hiring stops, therefore, when the value of the new output from new workers just covers the additional wages. When all producers reach this point, there is *equilibrium*.

What happens if prices go up? If wages don't do likewise, producers have an incentive to increase employment and output because the revenue received will more than cover the increase in the wage bill. Thus total output goes up when the price level goes up if wages do not change. (A big *if*, assuredly.)

Shifting now from aggregate supply to aggregate demand, we must back up to our discussion of the factors determining how much cash you want to hold. We said that historically people have kept cash on hand equal to some fairly stable proportion of their income. (Remember, for the time being we excluded the interest rate as a determinant of the public's desired money balances.) If people on average feel they have too much cash, their desired expenditures exceed output, so prices and/or output will rise until everyone is happy again. We can individually change the level of our cash balances, but together we have to hold all of the money supply provided by the monetary authorities. At full employment output cannot be increased. However, at less than full employment either prices or output or both can increase in response to desired expenditures exceeding income and output.

Equilibrium or peace of mind is generally restored when nominal income has increased to the point where people no longer think they have too much cash. Hence, for every total amount of cash balances provided us, there is a combination of real output and price level which when multiplied together result in a nominal income which makes us all happy with the amount of cash we're all holding. These various combinations of outputs and price levels result in equilibrium in the goods and services sector of the economy. Equilibrium, as always, occurs where supply equals demand. All of these equilibrium combinations of output-price level can be thought of as the aggregate demand relation we've been looking for; for any output in this relation, the corresponding price level will cause desired expenditures to equal output, *given a certain total supply of cash balances in existence.*

If the money supply is greater than the demand for money, individuals will attempt to reduce their money balances by spending more than their receipts. (They could, alternatively, burn it, as is done in an ancient Chinese ceremony.) Although in the aggregate individuals must hold the money supply created by the Federal Reserve and the commercial banks, the attempt to reduce their money balances creates excess demand for goods and services. If members of the private sector desire to spend more than their income in the attempt to reduce money balances, desired expenditures on goods and services will exceed output, since income must equal output. This excess demand for goods and services induces an increase in prices and/or output. The resulting increase in nominal income will increase the demand for money. The demand for goods and services will equal the supply of goods and services only when the demand for money equals the supply of money.

For every money supply, there are various combinations of outputs and price levels which make the demand for money equal to the supply of money. If a larger output is offered for sale, the price at which the output is sold will have to fall, because the increased real income generated from the sale of a larger output will increase the public's demand for *real money balances* (value of money balances expressed in terms of their purchasing power over goods and services). The real money balances increase as the price of goods and services falls. Consequently, given the stock of money, a larger output can be sold only at lower prices; this is our aggregate demand relationship. Again, for simplicity, it ignores completely the important role interest rates play in the demand for money.

We still don't know what output and price level will exist at any one time. In the simplified world outlined above, the answer will be given by finding, for a given wage rate and a given money supply, that combination which simultaneously satisfies producers and consumers.[1] At that nominal income (real output X the price level) consumers will be happy with their existing cash balances. At that level of output and prices producers will be employing as many workers and producing as much output as is profitable.

Suppose the price level were higher than that dictated by equilibrium. This higher price would reduce the purchasing power of existing cash balances; individuals would attempt to increase their money balances to make up this reduction of purchasing power. Desired expenditures would therefore be *less* than output and income as people attempted to build up their cash balances. Consequently, there would be excess supply of goods and services at that price level.

If the price level were too low, producers wouldn't want to supply the equilibrium output, because only the equilibrium price level makes it profitable for them to produce that much output. At the lower price producers would cut back on employment because the saving in the wages bill would exceed the lost revenue from not selling as much output. The *equilibrium price level* is just high enough to make it profitable for producers to supply the *equilibrium* output.

Now that we've given you some idea of what aggregate supply and demand depend on, let's see what would happen if, say, the money supply were to double. Something would have to give. Before the doubling you were happy with your cash balances. After the doubling you'd have to have "too much" cash. People would attempt all at once to get rid of these extra dollar bills. Alternatively, we could consider that a new aggregate demand relation would have to be established. For everyone to be perfectly happy with the new money supply, nominal income (price level X output) would also have to double. This can of course be accomplished by a doubling of the price level.

The current output would sell for twice the price, for that would be the price level at which the demand and supply of money would be equal. At a higher price level, however,

[1]At the intersection of the aggregate supply and demand curves.

producers would desire to expand their labor forces and increase output, for the increase in revenue from the sales of additional output would exceed the increase in labor costs. If the economy is already at full employment, producers will succeed in adding to their labor force only by bidding workers away from other producers: there will be no net increase in employment. The attempt by each producer to expand output will simply bid up the wage rate to twice its original level. A doubling of the money supply in this case will result in a new equilibrium with prices and wages doubling and output remaining the same.

On the other hand, if there are unemployed workers who offer their labor services at the current wage rate, producers will succeed in increasing aggregate output. Prices will rise, but they will not double, for the increased real income generated by the sale of additional output will increase the demand for real money balances.

The impact of a *decrease* in the money supply on employment depends upon the willingness of labor to accept wage cuts. Suppose the money supply were to fall by one-half. The same output could be sold only if prices fell by one-half, for that would be the price level which would make the supply and demand for money equal. Producers would find it profitable to continue to supply the current output at one-half the equilibrium price level only if wage rates were cut in half. If workers preferred to become unemployed rather than accept the wage cut, producers would reduce employment and output, for the savings in labor costs would exceed the loss of revenue. Rigid wage rates would result in reduced employment and output. Prices would fall, but by less than 50 percent because the fall in real income resulting from reduced employment and output would reduce the demand for real money balances.

These aggregate demand and supply relationships can now be used to explain the behavior of output and prices since 1960. The above analysis was *static* because we were not talking about a *dynamic* adjustment to a growing economy and money supply. Instead of the stock of money change, we shall now discuss changes in the *rate* of monetary growth.

The increase in output from 1961 to 1965 (at a 5.4 percent annual rate) was possible because there were unemployed resources when the expansion started. During this period wage rates continued to expand at a fairly slow rate. Unit labor costs were rising at only 1.3 percent a year during the period. Consequently the expansion in GNP (at 6.8 percent annually), resulting in part from a moderate expansion in the money supply (at a 3 percent annual rate), occurred primarily as an expansion of output rather than as inflation. The rate of inflation averaged only 1.4 percent a year.

In 1965, the money supply growth rate accelerated to a 6.6 percent annual rate, partly to finance increased military expenditures in Vietnam. As could be expected, gross national product also accelerated (to a 9.3 percent annual rate during 1965 and early 1966). As a result of the rapid expansion in employment since 1961, the economy was very close to full employment. The burst of gross national product growth during 1965 and early 1966 had to occur primarily in the form of inflation, since the growth of real output was limited by the full-employment situation. Inflation accelerated to a 3.5 percent annual rate during the first half of 1966.

This acceleration of inflation scared the Federal Reserve into slowing down the rate of monetary growth. Some observers have called this episode "the Fed's finest hour," because it demonstrated the Fed's independence of the President. President Johnson protested this slowdown in the rate of monetary growth. In fact the President called William McChesney Martin, then Chairman of the Board of Governors of the Federal Reserve System, down to the Ranch to persuade him to change his monetary policy. However, the Federal Reserve was determined to slow the rate of monetary growth, and that they did. During the last three quarters of 1966 the money supply actually *fell* slightly. The mini-recession of late 1966 and early 1967 was the result. GNP growth slowed to a 3.3 percent annual rate. Prices continued to rise at over 2.5 percent because of wage increases that were induced by expectations of continuing inflation, and therefore output could only expand at a 0.6 percent annual rate. Unemployment started to rise.

Just as the Federal Reserve had overreacted to the inflation in 1965, now it overreacted to the rise in unemployment. From 1967 to 1969 the money supply grew at the extremely rapid rate of 7.6 percent a year. The result was an inflation we are still trying to contain. By 1969 prices were rising at over 6 percent a year.

In 1969 the Federal Reserve finally restrained the rate of monetary growth in two steps. From January to July of 1969, the annual rate of growth in the money supply was reduced to 5.1 percent. From July to December of 1969 the money supply slowed substantially to a mere 0.6 percent annual rate of growth. Following that drastic decrease in the rate of growth in the money supply, the slowdown in economic activity beginning in the fourth quarter of 1969 was to be expected. When total spending does slow down, there is usually a lag before inflation starts to slow. This is because labor costs, reflecting inflationary expectations consistent with the previous rate of expansion of aggregate nominal demand,[2] continue to rise for some time after the growth in GNP slows. Since prices continued to rise at about 6 percent a year, output had to fall and unemployment increased.

From February 1970 to January 1971 the Federal Reserve increased the money supply at about a 6 percent annual rate. At the same time growth in GNP accelerated, and output started to expand again. The expansion was a moderate one, not vigorous enough to reduce the unemployment rate. The Federal Reserve (under Chairman Arthur Burns) faced the cruel dilemma of choosing between higher inflation and high unemployment in early 1971. President Nixon was uneasy about the effects of lingering unemployment on his 1972

[2]Aggregate nominal demand is meant, throughout this book, to mean desired total spending on goods and services.

election. The Federal Reserve was under pressure to stimulate the economy by increasing the rate of monetary growth. Evidently the Fed responded to that pressure, because the money supply increased at over 10 percent a year during the first half of 1971.

In the summer of 1971 the Fed, Congress, and the President faced the specter of more inflation. If the rate of GNP growth were stimulated too fast, most of that growth would be in the form of increased rates of inflation.

You have probably noticed from this discussion that the government always seems to be faced with the unpleasant choice between higher inflation and higher unemployment. This supposed trade-off between inflation and unemployment is the subject of our next chapter.

# 8

## THE ECONOMICS
## OF THE INFLATIONARY
## RECESSION

The United States in 1971 was still in the midst of an annoying phenomenon—an inflationary recession. Most people can't understand why prices can be rising at rapid rates with unemployment at such high levels (6 percent). Usually, we have been taught to associate rising prices and wages with rising employment. Now people are beginning to doubt that even a recession can reduce the rate of inflation.

Since one of the goals of the Federal Reserve and the Council of Economic Advisors is to produce and maintain full employment, in early 1971 these policy makers were confronted with the difficult choice between an increase in the rate of inflation and unacceptably high unemployment. The relationship between unemployment and inflation was empirically documented by A. A. Phillips and as a result is known as the *Phillips curve*. The Phillips curve implies that there is a trade-off between inflation and unemployment. Stable prices presumably must be paid for by high unemployment. Monetary policy should be expansionary enough to generate an "acceptable" amount of inflation in order to keep unemployment at "tolerable" levels.

Unfortunately, the Phillips curve relationship has not proved very stable over time. Professors Mary Hamilton and Albert Rees commented in a study of this relationship: " . . . we regard the construction of a plausible Phillips curve from annual data for a long period of time as a *tour de force* somewhat comparable to writing the Lord's Prayer on the head of a pin, rather than as a guide to policy." They concluded: " . . . the authors of Phillips curves would do well to label them conspicuously 'Unstable—Apply with extreme care.' " Since 1965 the maintenance of a given unemployment rate has required progressively higher rates of inflation. The trade-off between unemployment and inflation has become increasingly worse. The source of the instability was alluded to in the last chapter. The problem with the original Phillips curve analysis is that it completely ignores people's *expectations* of future inflation. The impact of changes in that expected rate of inflation has extremely important effects on the trade-off between inflation and unemployment.

If the rate of wage and price inflation were fully anticipated at every moment in time, output would be affected very little by changes in the rate of growth of nominal aggregate demand. Real output would increase at its equilibrium growth rate and the remaining growth in nominal income (GNP) required to equate the demand and supply of money would be in the form of inflation. Changes in the rate of growth of nominal aggregate demand would simply result in a new rate of inflation.

In the long run when the actual rate of inflation is anticipated, real output is independent of the rate of growth of nominal aggregate demand. In the short run, however, changes in the rate of growth of nominal aggregate demand do have important effects on output and employment. Temporary fluctuations in output and employment result from unfulfilled expectations that occur during the period of adjustment to the new, previously unanticipated, rate of inflation.

When the rate of growth of nominal aggregate demand is

reduced, for some time economic decisions will be based upon false expectations of a higher rate of wage and price inflation. Union leaders will therefore continue to seek higher wages to protect workers' earnings from incorrectly expected continued inflation. Business firms, likewise, will expect to meet these wage demands through price increases. Since the rate of growth of nominal aggregate demand has slowed, the higher wages negotiated for in labor contracts based on the incorrect inflationary expectations will result in reduced employment in the unionized sector of the economy. The producer expects to be able to pass the increased labor costs on in higher prices. But nominal aggregate demand will be too low to generate sufficient demand to purchase the output at that price. Consequently, employment and output will fall. In the nonunionized sector, where wages are contracted for shorter periods of time than in the unionized sector, wage rate offers will rise at a slower rate as the growth in nominal aggregate demand slows. The gap that develops between the actual and expected wage rates induces unemployed individuals to reject current wage offers and remain unemployed in the expectation of receiving higher offers. The unemployed workers will "overinvest" in the search for higher wages, increasing the average duration of unemployment.

During this period of adjustment to a lower rate of inflation, aggregate unemployment temporarily increases for a period of time because of the gap between actual wage and price levels and their expected levels. In the above simplified world there is no long-run trade-off between inflation and unemployment, for expectations (forecasts) eventually adjust to reality. The rise in the average duration of unemployment forces the unemployed labor force to readjust their expectations. Any stable rate of growth of nominal aggregate demand will permit the equilibrium rate of inflation to be fully anticipated. When inflation is anticipated, the unemployment rate will stabilize at its long-run natural rate.

Individuals moving from one job to another have some desired or optimal period of search for job offers. Very few individuals will accept the first job offered them unless it exceeds the forecast wage offer they expect to receive if they remain unemployed and continue to search. Each individual may receive wage offers above or below the average value of market wage rates. If he correctly anticipates this average value, he will invest the "correct" amount of time in his search for another job. This search for job offers creates a stable long-run normal unemployment rate, sometimes called *frictional unemployment*.

An increase in the rate of inflation can produce a temporary reduction in the unemployment rate below its long-run normal level, but this temporary reduction in unemployment does not imply an improvement in economic welfare. Suppose, for example, that the rate of inflation accelerates. Economic decisions made during the period of adjustment of forecasts to the new rate of inflation will reflect expectations of a lower rate of inflation consistent with a slower rate of growth of nominal aggregate demand. The nominal value of wage offers will rise more rapidly than expected. Unemployed individuals will receive, on average, higher wage offers than they had expected to receive. The failure to anticipate the increased inflation will induce individuals to accept job offers earlier than if they had anticipated the acceleration of inflation. The average duration of unemployment will fall, but this reduction in unemployment will not increase economic welfare in the long run. Labor can increase its real wages (wages expressed in terms of purchasing power over goods and services) only by increasing productivity. One important source of advances in productivity is the movement of workers from sectors of the economy where labor productivity is low to sectors where productivity is high. The search for job offers is the process by which workers discover areas where their productivity is highest. If the actual average value of wage offers exceeds its expected value, workers will underinvest in the search for new job offers. So although an acceleration in the rate of inflation can reduce the unemployment rate below its long-run normal level, the rate of productivity growth will be reduced, since workers will underinvest in the search for the occupation where productivity is highest.

To maintain an unemployment rate below its long-run normal level, the actual rate of inflation must exceed its expected rate. Expectations will, however, adjust to reality. To maintain a gap between the actual and expected rates would require an accelerating rate of inflation to stay ahead of readjustments in the expected rate of inflation. Consequently, there is probably no long-run trade-off between inflation and unemployment. An accelerating inflation which is always underestimated is required to keep the unemployment rate below the equilibrium level forever.

# 9

## THE ECONOMICS OF LABOR UNIONS AND INFLATION: ROOSEVELT'S ECONOMIC GAME PLAN FOR THE GREAT DEPRESSION

By the time Franklin D. Roosevelt took office the nation had seen output fall by 36 percent since 1929. One of Roosevelt's first duties as President, as he saw it, was to raise prices. For the farm sector the Agricultural Adjustment Act was passed in 1933. The Agricultural Adjustment Administration was set up to raise prices by restrictions on the supply of crops. The AAA created the Commodity Credit Corporation and with it a system of agricultural price supports and acreage restrictions, the vestiges of which are still with us today.

Roosevelt also succeeded in passing the National Industrial Recovery Act. He hoped it would allow industries, through collusion and cartelization, to raise prices and give businessmen more incentives to produce.

The dominant theory behind the act was that industrial depression could be reduced by getting rid of "wasteful, cutthroat competition." This was to be accomplished by establishing management organizations to collude on prices and quantities and by encouraging organization among the workers.

The act was originally intended to apply only to big

industries, but the NRA (National Recovery Administration) became ambitious and soon established a universally applied blanket code known as the President's Re-employment Agreement (Blue Eagle). The NRA approved over 500 codes of operation for various industries. These codes were drawn up by the industrialists. Employers dominated the administrative body of the NRA. In most cases the codes were never enforced and collusion didn't work.

The NRA also was supposed to grant "justice to the worker." Section 7a allowed for the right of labor to bargain collectively. Roosevelt believed that the way to cure the Depression was to increase wages. His supporting argument sounds plausible on the surface. He reasoned that if wages are increased, the income of labor is increased, thereby allowing workers to buy more goods and services. If laborers buy more goods and services, that increased demand will result in a demand for additional workers. This argument has remained popular, particularly with labor unions. But there is a flaw in the argument which we discuss below.

When the NRA was declared unconstitutional, Section 7a was replaced by the much more extensive Wagner Act (National Labor Relations Act). The premise behind this act was that the inequality in bargaining power between workers as individuals and large businesses depresses "the purchasing power of wage earners in industry" and prevents "stabilization of competitive wage rates and working conditions." The act guaranteed workers the right to start labor unions, to be members in them, and to engage in collective bargaining. The Wagner Act, in addition, outlined a long list of "uniform" labor practices.

The Wagner Act was indeed labor's Magna Charta. After the Supreme Court declared it constitutional in 1937, organized labor rapidly grew in strength in our economy.

Was Roosevelt successful in raising prices? While the money supply increased at an annual rate of 11 percent from 1933 to 1937, prices increased at an incredible 13 percent a year while output went up only about 1 percent a year.

Unemployment remained high. It should not have been surprising, though. With any given increase in the money supply, the more prices increase, the less output will increase because the inflation will reduce the purchasing power of those money balances. As the purchasing power of money balances is reduced by inflation, individuals will desire to maintain larger nominal money balances. Of course, the desire to increase nominal money balances is translated into the desire to reduce spending on goods and services relative to income because of each individual's budget constraint.[1] The inflation, then, will reduce the amount of output individuals will desire to purchase out of their income. Roosevelt's game plan succeeded in raising prices, but in so doing it prevented output from responding to rapid monetary and fiscal expansion. Perhaps it was during this period in American history that the idea originated that labor unions cause inflation. This is perhaps true for the Depression's 5-year period, but we shall attempt to demonstrate why it can't be true for any long-run period.

Before doing that let's look at the state of unionism in the U.S. today. Less of the labor force is unionized here than in most industrial countries. Sweden and Britain can both boast that more than 40 percent of their labor force is unionized. On the other hand, only 22 percent of the U.S. labor force belongs to organized labor.

Back in 1953 26 percent of our labor force was unionized. This figure fell to about 24 percent for the rest of the fifties. Then by 1961 it was almost 23 percent and has fallen gradually since. The reasons for such a reversed trend in unionization of the U.S. labor force are many, but several stand out. There has been a rapid growth in the service (or tertiary) sector of the economy. It has been very difficult for unions to organize in the services. Today less than 10 percent of all service workers belong to unions.

In addition, much of the gains in manufacturing employ-

[1]Any individual can increase his money balances only by spending less than his receipts.

ment have involved increased white-collar employment. Only about 15 percent of all white-collar workers are in unions.

The fact that unionism has been waning and *not* waxing should already make you suspicious of unions' ability to cause a sustained inflation such as we have right now. Analytically, labor unions cannot be the source of a sustained inflation merely by increasing wages unless the monetary authorities permit a rapid expansion of the money supply to accompany the rise in wages. Suppose some industry becomes unionized and the union succeeds in increasing the wage rate. Each producer is attempting to maximize his profits by expanding output to the point at which the increase in total revenue produced by additional workers is equal to the increase in labor costs associated with hiring those workers. If the union is successful in raising the wage rate, and nominal aggregate demand does not increase, producers will find it profitable to lay off workers and reduce output, since the savings in labor costs will exceed the reduction in total revenue resulting from the fall in output. Employment will fall in the unionized industry. The reduction in output and employment raises the price of the output and increases the marginal productivity of labor. Employment and output will stabilize when the lost revenue from further layoffs equals the savings in labor costs.

In the short run higher prices in the unionized industry increase the general index of prices and aggregate output, and employment falls. Eventually, however, the unemployed workers will find employment in other sectors of the economy. As unemployed workers drive down wages in other industries, producers have an incentive to expand output, reducing prices. Thus, no significant change in the over-all price level will occur.

Unions can successfully increase wage rates above the nonunion level only by destroying job opportunities in their industry. Most unions have not succeeded in increasing the wages of their workers above the nonunion level; they have merely received credit for wage gains which would have occurred even in the absence of unions. A few unions have succeeded in increasing wage rates by restricting the supply of labor to the industry, primarily through licensing and apprenticeship requirements.

There is one situation where unions can raise wages without affecting employment in that industry. It involves infamous company towns where there is only one source of employment for a large area. Here the sole employer can act as a monopolist[2] in the hiring of labor. A union can walk into such a situation and force wages up without causing the single employer to reduce hirings because that employer will have been paying less than the value of each employee's marginal product to start with.

On a world basis, unionism and inflation don't seem to be related. In 1970 unit labor costs in Britain jumped up 10.6 percent while they increased 13 percent in West Germany. The former is almost 50 percent more unionized than the latter. Wages in Sweden and France both climbed 11 percent in 1970. The Swedish labor force is almost 300 percent more unionized than is the French.

Don't get the impression that wages can't be kept up by unions in certain sectors, especially with government help. The construction industry is a good example. Its union members are aided by the Walsh-Healy and Davis-Bacon Acts which were passed during the Depression. These acts require all contractors working on projects even partially funded by the government to pay the workers on the projects "prevailing wages." In a futile attempt at slowing the rate of inflation the administration briefly suspended the Davis-Bacon Act in 1971. This action certainly did not earn many friends in the building trade union, as might have been expected.

Whatever your individual feelings are about unions, unions have not recently become all-powerful, and they cannot cause a *sustained* inflation.

[2]Actually, a monopsonist.

# THE ECONOMICS OF WAGE
# AND PRICE CONTROLS: HOW
# TO MAKE CIGARETTES A CURRENCY

In a *Playboy* interview some years ago, Professor John Kenneth Galbraith told about his days with the Office of Price Administration during World War II. At one point in the interview Dr. Galbraith said he had decided during one trying moment in those war-torn years that it might be easier for a price of $5.00 to be set on *everything*. Such a radical idea is proof enough that the job of keeping the lid on prices during World War II must not have been easy.

The desire to control prices did not, of course, disappear after the end of hostilities. We've had "jawboning" from at least four Presidents since then, official "guideposts," a temporary price and wage freeze, and other controls.

In World War II the pressure of huge government expenditures (initially payed for largely by increasing the money supply) and full employment were sure to bring about rising prices. Congress was only willing to raise taxes to cover 61 percent of its expenditures. The Price Control Act of January 1942 established the Office of Price Administration. By mid-1943 fully 95 percent of the nation's foodstuffs were rationed, and maximum prices and rents had been established.

The Anti-inflation Act of October 1942 established the Office of Economic Stabilization. Its purpose was to limit wages and salaries and curb prices and rents not yet controlled. At the height of price controls, these two offices, along with the Office of War Mobilization, created in 1943, were aided by about 350,000 volunteer "price watchers" scattered throughout the country. This enormous nationwide effort resulted in wholesale prices rising only 14 percent from November 1941 to August 1945.[1]

Nazi Germany also controlled prices, even more drastically than the U.S. So-called economic crimes such as selling products above the maximum legal price were immediately dealt with in a much harsher manner than in America. When the Allies occupied Germany after the war, they didn't dismantle the rationing scheme. It was felt that chaos would have resulted. For 3 years strict price controls were effectively enforced because Germany was an occupied country. During that same period available cash balances grew a phenomenal 400 percent. Output, however, fell by 50 percent. Barter developed as the German mark became useless, since the mark could no longer be used to obtain goods and services because of widespread shortages. Believe it or not, American cigarettes became the unofficial currency.

Obviously, price controls in postwar Germany were much more successful than in postwar America. They were so successful that the official price index hardly budged at all.

It might be interesting at this point to see what happened in post-World War I Germany. The Allies, using the Treaty of Versailles, had imposed immense reparation payments on that country. In order to finance these payments the Weimar Republic printed marks, lots of them. By 1923 the German government was spending 12 *billion* marks more than it was receiving in taxes. Its expenditures were 7 times as great as its revenues. The mark/U.S. dollar exchange rate went as fol-

[1]However, when the war and controls ended, the story changed. The wholesale price index jumped 55 percent from August 1945 to August 1948.

lows: 1919—14; 1920—40; 1920—77; 1923—353,412. From July 1923 to November 1923, the mark/dollar rate went from 353,412 to 4,200,000,000. Since there weren't any price controls then, retail prices and wages adjusted rapidly to the influx of marks. In the end there were *hourly* changes in prices!

In contrast to the reduction in output in post-World War II Germany, output in post-World War I Germany did not fall until the last 6 months of inflation, when people started resorting to barter.

The juxtaposition of these periods in German history is perhaps useful to demonstrate what can happen during periods of phenomenal increases in the amount of available cash balances—with and without price controls.

If the money supply increases rapidly, the public's attempt to get rid of their excess money balances produces excess demand for goods and services. Market prices will rise until the demand for money equals the supply of money. If price controls prevent prices from rising, the excess demand for goods and services becomes apparent as shortages develop. At the legal price level, the demand for goods will exceed the supply of goods, requiring an alternative method of rationing the available supply. Individuals hold money balances in order to have a liquid stock of purchasing power over goods and services. If there are widespread shortages due to excess demand for goods and services, money is no longer a liquid stock of purchasing power over goods and services. Money balances can no longer perform the services for which they have been held. The resort to barter or the creation of a new commodity currency, such as cigarettes, naturally follows.

If nationwide wage and price controls are effectively enforced during a period in which the money supply increases rapidly, people will eventually refuse to accept legal tender in exchange. Shortages will destroy the usefulness of legal tender and force individuals to resort to barter or to the invention of a commodity currency medium of exchange for which there are no price controls.

Post-World War II Germany essentially experienced a complete destruction of its monetary standard. After price controls were lifted, a new banking system was instituted, and the Marshall Plan got rolling, West Germany experienced what has been called a miracle. Between 1948 and 1964 industrial production increased 600 percent. Real GNP tripled between 1950 and 1964. Per capita GNP in real terms increased faster in West Germany than in any other Western European or North American country. Of course this experience was a miracle only to those who did not understand the destructiveness of price controls in the earlier period.

There has been little support since the forties for full-fledged price controls in this country, except for a brief while during the Korean conflict. The concept of informal guidelines or guideposts has been given a lot of attention, though. Every *Economic Report of the President and the Council of Economic Advisors* since 1957 has stressed, in one form or another, that private pricing discretion should be tempered to create stable prices. Restraint on the part of business and workers has been requested. The 1960 *Economic Report* was explicit in stating that wage increases should not exceed the growth in average *national* productivity. It further suggested that price reductions were called for in sectors experiencing exceptionally rapid productivity growth.

The 1962 *Report* gave us a formal statement of guideposts for wage increases. They should not exceed about 3.5 percent, which was the rate of growth of productivity in the economy.

Presidents Kennedy, Johnson, and Nixon attempted to roll back specific price increases by jawboning and sometimes by explicit threats. Kennedy got U.S. Steel to rescind a price increase in 1962 by making it a national issue.

Dr. Arthur F. Burns of the Federal Reserve in late 1970 suggested the creation of a "high level price and review board, which, while lacking enforcement powers, would have broad authority to investigate, advise, and recommend on price and wage changes."

The idea behind such measures is obvious: we could then have higher rates of employment without the odious consequences of rising prices. While the debate is not yet exhausted on this idea, there is a place for guidelines consistent with a theory we presented before about the adjustment period between rising prices and stable prices.

Monetary and fiscal policy from 1967 to 1969 was extremely expansionary. It abruptly changed in 1969 and was much less expansionary until early 1971. During this period of adjustment and concomitant high unemployment, people still expected high rates of inflation. After all, businessmen had learned to expect that they could raise prices without decreasing sales. Union workers had just suffered a period of little *real* change in wages. It would have been very difficult for all concerned to suddenly accept the idea that there was a permanent decrease in the growth of nominal aggregate demand.

Here's where guidelines come in. If they were to be established in order to signal a permanent or long-term change in government monetary and fiscal policy which would be consistent with stable prices, then wage and price controls might speed up the adjustment of expectations we explained in Chapter 8.

However, the structure of prices would probably be seriously distorted by price and wage fixing legislation, producing shortages of some goods and misallocation of resources. The best method for speeding up the adjustment of expectations to changing rates of inflation would be contracts negotiated in *real* terms rather than *nominal* terms. Workers and management could sign contracts linking wage rates to a cost of living index, thus eliminating the problems associated with forecasting future inflation. Wages would then go up rapidly only if there were inflation. If prices remained stable, the rise in wage rates would simply reflect the agreed upon growth in real purchasing power. The authors feel that the use of such contracts would contribute significantly to stable growth in output. They could virtually eliminate the phenomenon of an inflationary recession.

It is doubtful now whether guidelines will ever be respected by labor and business. Monetary policy went wild in early 1971 and the government was running a large deficit. It's hard to imagine people believing that prices would stabilize when the money supply was being expanded at 12 percent a year and the government deficit was to exceed $20 billion.

# 11

## THE ECONOMICS
## OF MINIMUM WAGES:
## HOW TO KEEP THE SOUTH DOWN

The debate about raising the minimum wage from $1.60 an hour to $2.00 was hotly contested by Congress in June 1971. Leon Keyserling, a former chairman of the Council of Economic Advisors, stated that a higher minimum wage was essential to provide the consumer purchasing power needed to increase total spending in the economy. Paul Samuelson, winner of the Nobel Prize in economics, objected: "What good does it do a black youth to know that an employer must pay him $1.60 an hour if the fact that he must be paid that amount is what keeps him from getting a job?" Milton Friedman called the minimum wage law "the most anti-Negro law on our statute books—in its effect, not its intent."

The desire for minimum wages isn't new. It started before the turn of the century. Minimum wage legislation grew out of the general movement against the "exploitation of the poor working girl" and low pay for workers toiling in bad working conditions. Agitation for better conditions developed out of inquiries into existing working standards and wages. Until 1912 the movement for a minimum wage produced very little result. In that year, though, Massachusetts passed a "moral suasion" law to compel employers to pay standard wage rates. These rates were to be established by a state wage board. Any employer who did not comply with the standard would have his name published. In 1913 eight more states passed minimum wage laws. Seven of these states made the minimum wage rate compulsory. However, the laws applied only to women and minors and left totally unaffected the bulk of workers at that time.

It was not until the New Deal's National Industrial Recovery Act in 1933 that a federal minimum wage was set. At that time the rate was between 30¢ and 40¢ an hour. When the NIRA was declared unconstitutional in 1937 so, too, were the minimum wages established under it. Within a year, though, the Fair Labor Standards Act established a minimum wage of 25¢ for all industries which were involved in interstate commerce. This act has remained the basis for the current federal minimum wage. The national minimum wage went to 30¢ in 1939. By 1945 it was 40¢ an hour. In 1950 it was raised to 75¢ and in 1956 it was again raised to $1.00 an hour. Since then it has increased in several steps: $1.15 an hour, $1.25 an hour, to the current $1.60 an hour rate.

Economists analyze the effects of an increase in the minimum wage by applying the *derived demand relationship*. The demand for labor by employers depends upon the wage rate and the price at which *output* is sold. Each employer has an incentive (profit maximization) to hire additional workers as long as the increased revenue generated by an additional worker is greater than the increase in labor costs. Employers, in the aggregate, hire workers up to the point where the value of the additional output made possible by the new workers just equals the increase in the employer's wage bill. If the wage rate is arbitrarily increased by government edict, some marginal workers become unprofitable to employ. Profit maximization had induced some employers to hire marginal workers because they just produced goods whose market value would just enable the employer to pay the going wage. If nominal aggregate demand remains constant, at the higher wage rate employers can no longer afford to employ those marginal workers, for the market value of their contribution to total output is less than the minimum wage rate.

Producers cannot raise prices to finance the increased wages of all those marginal workers because at higher prices, less output will be purchased by consumers. Part of the labor force becomes redundant if sales fall off.

Those marginal workers who lose their jobs do not receive the minimum wage. They receive no wage. Of course they may find jobs elsewhere in sectors of the economy that are not covered by the minimum wage legislation. To induce employers in those sectors to hire additional workers, though, wage rates there must fall. By eliminating marginal job opportunities, the minimum wage hurts the very people it was intended to help.

There are some situations in which an increase in the minimum wage will not, theoretically, bring about unemployment. For example, we refer to the company towns. When an employer acts as a monopsonist he realizes that if he wishes to hire additional laborers he must pay higher wages. (He faces a distinctly upward sloping supply curve of labor because he is the only employer.)

If the monopsonist must pay all of his workers the same wage rate, any time he raises wages to attract a new employee he must increase everyone's wage. The marginal cost of increasing employment consists of the additional wages paid to the new workers plus the increment in the wages that must be paid to all existing workers. The monopsonist will not hire the marginal worker unless the value of his contribution to output is equal to the total increase in labor costs necessary to hire him—his wage rate plus the increment in wages paid to all existing workers. Consequently, the monopsonist will not pay his workers the full value of their (marginal) product. If the government legislates a minimum wage which is high enough to produce a supply of workers who are willing to work at the minimum wage rate, the employer will be able to hire additional workers without increasing the wages of the existing labor force because they already must be paid the minimum wage. The marginal costs associated with hiring an additional individual actually may fall even though the wage rate rises because the new minimum wage legislation means that the wages of current workers no longer need to be increased to attract additional workers. If the cost of hiring additional workers falls because of the minimum wage, the monopsonist will have an incentive to hire more workers. Maximum employment in the company town will occur when the minimum wage is equal to the level of wages which would exist in a competitive situation.

This argument is not taken seriously, however, for two reasons. There are few situations where an employer's employment decisions could affect wages significantly. There is just too much competition between employers for labor. Moreover, even if there were monopsonistic employers, they could probably devise a scheme to confine the higher wage rate to marginal employees without having to raise the wages of their existing labor force.

Even in a normal situation where monopsony elements are not present, an increase in the minimum wage does not harm everyone. As a matter of fact there are some workers (in addition to those receiving the new minimum wage rates) who will benefit. When the minimum wage is increased, those workers who are no longer profitably employed by some employers are the ones who contribute the least to the total output. These are, for example, the unskilled, the aged, the uneducated. Unskilled workers can be substituted for skilled workers. The demand for skilled labor increases when the price of its substitute increases. Therefore when an increase in the minimum wage forces some lower-skilled workers out of an industry, it increases the demand for higher-skilled workers.

Many people cannot understand how an increase in the minimum wage can possibly affect *total* employment. It is argued that a few cents' increase in required wages will not cause employers to lay off any of their employees. To be sure, a small change in the minimum wage will not be translated into any noticeable change in employment. On the other hand, given a sufficiently large change in the minimum wage, some increased unemployment will ensue unless nominal aggregate demand is also increased. The Secretary of Labor is required by law to report to Congress each year on the effects of the minimum wage. In 1956, for example, the increase in the minimum wage was a substantial jump from 75¢ to $1.00 an hour. That is equivalent to a one-third increase. In 1959, a report by the Secretary of Labor concluded that "there were significant declines in employment in most of the low wage industries studied," after the increase in the minimum wage in 1956. Certainly we would not have expected to see such a noticeable decrease in employment when the minimum wage was increased from $1.15 to $1.25 in 1963. That is only a less than one-tenth increase in the minimum wage. In a growing economy it is very difficult to recognize how much unemployment is caused by such a small change in government regulated wages.

The evidence about the effects of minimum wages is quite impressive with respect to the teenage labor force. Teenagers in general have the lowest productivity in the economy. They have the least schooling and the least experience. Therefore, *a priori*, we would expect that they would be affected most by the minimum wage. From 1950 to 1956 white teenage unemployment ranged between 11 percent and 6.5 percent. After the minimum wage was raised in 1956 to $1.00, white teenage unemployment shot up from 7 percent to almost 14 percent. It has remained in excess of 12 percent ever since then. If one looks at nonwhite teenagers, mostly blacks, the effects of the minimum wage are even more striking. When that wage rate increase of one-third was effected in 1956, nonwhite teenage unemployment jumped from 13 percent to over 24 percent! In 1971 over-all teenage unemployment was 17.2 percent as opposed to 6.1 percent for the entire labor force. In a 1965 study by Dr. Arthur F. Burns the conclusion was reached that "the ratio of the unemployment rate of teenagers to that of male adults was invariably higher during the six months following an increase in the minimum wage than it was in the preceding half year."

Another effect of minimum wages is to increase the amount of automation in the economy. Automation brought about by artificially inflated wage rates does not necessarily mean that machines will replace men. Rather, those workers who produce machines are replacing those workers who do jobs without the machines. We have seen that historically it is unskilled workers who do jobs without machines. When their wage rates are forced up by increases in the minimum wage, it behooves employers to rely more heavily on the skilled workers who produce machines.

It is interesting to note which groups in the economy have pushed hardest for increases in the minimum wage. The most outspoken groups have consistently been unions and managements in northern industries. Since wages in those industries would not be directly affected by the minimum wage because they have always been well above it, it might seem that these unions and managements are looking out for the good of other workers. The fact is that unions and managements in northern industries favor increasing minimum wages in order to retard the movement of industry to the South. One of the greatest inducements for industry to move from the North to the South has been the possibility of hiring southern workers at lower wages than northern workers. Therefore, if unions and management in the North can effectively get the federal government to prohibit workers from being hired at lower wages in the South, very little industry will be induced to move from the North to the South. This point was brought out very clearly by Senator Jacob Javits of New York in the *Congressional Record* of February 23, 1966 (p. 2692):

> I point to Senators from industrial states like my own that a minimum wage increase would also give industry in our states some measure of protection as we have too long suffered from the unfair competition based on substandard wages and other

labor conditions in effect in certain areas of the country—primarily in the South.

The Senator from New York was applying the same logic to justify the minimum wage as certain American industrialists have used in order to justify the imposition of tariffs. An increase in the minimum wage increases the cost of producing goods being exported from the South to the North. Manufacturers and workers in the North favor this tarifflike device in order to protect themselves from southern competition.

In spite of the fact that the evidence presented above is only a small part of the total amount available which demonstrates the pernicious effects of large increases in the minimum wage, most Americans still favor this type of legislation. In a 1965 Gallup Poll, fully 55 percent of all those sampled thought the minimum wage should be raised. Perhaps a better reading of the historical record would dissuade some of these Americans from imposing the unemployment effects of increased minimum wages on our society.

# 12
## THE ECONOMICS
## OF SKY-HIGH
## INTEREST RATES

Rep. Wright Patman, Chairman of the House Banking and Currency Committee, has on numerous occasions called for federal legislation to fix interest charges. For example, the prime rate should be fixed low enough "to encourage expansion and production," he once said in 1971. His and others' concern over interest rates has rarely been as great as now because we are currently facing the highest interest rates since the Civil War.

High-grade corporate bond yields reached almost 9 percent in 1970. The last time they were anywhere near this level was in 1857. These rates stayed around 6.5 percent during the Civil War, fell drastically to 4.5 percent by 1864; they rose again and stayed high until 1874, then slowly fell to 3 percent by 1900. The next 20 years saw a gradual increase to almost 6 percent, then a drastic decline in interest rates during the Great Depression. The rate was not much above 2 percent at the end of World War II. The postwar trend has obviously been upward in spite of some downturns in 1954, 1958, 1960, and 1966.

Interest rates have moved cyclically with the business

cycle. They have generally fallen in recessions and depressions. The current situation is somewhat of an exception to the historical record. We'll try to explain why in a moment.

When we talk about "the" interest rate we, of course, realize that there is no one single rate. Wright Patman likes to look at the *prime* rate. This is the interest rate charged very large corporations (which have impeccable financial credentials) for all the money they borrow. The prime rate is usually lower than all other interest rates because there is very little risk of nonrepayment involved. GM is not going to go bankrupt next year.[1] Few expenses are incurred by the banks lending large sums of money to such big corporate giants—no credit checks and the like.

The published prime rate can be misleading, though. In recent periods of high inflation, banks have required *compensatory balances* as one requirement to obtain a loan. Suppose the General Motors Acceptance Corporation wants a $10 million loan from Chase Manhattan. Assume Chase agrees to issue the loan at the published 6 percent prime rate. Suppose it requires GMAC to leave $5 million in a non-interest-bearing checking account. The true interest payment is $600,000 for borrowing effectively only $5 million. That is, GMAC would end up paying 12 percent and not the published 6 percent. Unless one knows what compensatory balances are required for any type of bank loan, one cannot be sure that the reported interest rate is the actual interest charge paid.

There are other long-term interest rates in the economy; we talked about the history of one of the high-grade corporate bond interest rates. This is usually referred to as the Aaa (triple A) rate, in reference to the highest grade listing bestowed on corporate bonds by Moody's Investment Service. There are also the municipal bond rates, long-term U.S. government bond rates and the 3- to 5-year government rate.

Shorter term rates include 90-day U.S. treasury bills, 4- to

[1]Rolls-Royce did, though, so big business size does not guarantee eternal financial stability.

6-month commercial paper, prime bankers' acceptances, and 90-day certificates of deposits.

All interest rates have one thing in common: they represent the price charged by the issuer of the loan for giving to the receiver of the loan command over goods and services today. This price varies depending on the length of the loan, the risks involved, and the expected change in the purchasing power of the money involved over the loan's life.

Interest rates have had a special place in economic theory. Since the cost of capital is a large part of the total cost of any businessman's investment, a change in the cost of capital represented by an increase in the interest rate should reduce aggregate investment. Economic theory suggests then that rising interest rates lead to a contraction of economic activity, and decreasing rates have the converse effect. However, historically interest rates have conformed very closely and positively with the business cycle; moreover, the secular rise in interest rates has accompanied the secular rise in income.

John Maynard Keynes named this phenomenon "Gibson's Paradox" after A. H. Gibson, who wrote about it in 1923. Keynes and others attempted to explain the paradox, but Irving Fisher had already analyzed the problem in 1896. Fisher, besides working doggedly for temperance, pointed out the distinction between the *nominal*, or market, rate of interest and the *real* rate of interest.

Nominal, or market, interest rates measure the rate of exchange between current and future dollars. (One dollar exchanges for $1 + i$ dollars 1 year hence, where i is the nominal interest rate.) Savings and investment decisions, however, should depend on the *real rate of interest* (the nominal interest rate minus the expected rate of price change). The real interest rate measures the rate of exchange between current and future goods and services.

For example, if there is no current or expected inflation, the nominal rate is identical to the real rate. The rate of exchange between current and future dollars is the same as the rate of exchange between current and future goods, because it takes the same number of dollars to purchase each good in both time periods. Assume that, all of a sudden, prices start increasing at 3 percent a year and this rate of inflation is expected to last indefinitely. If the real rate of interest is, say, 3 percent, the nominal rate of interest must rise to 6 percent, because it will take more dollars to purchase each good in the future.

Remember in the first chapter we discussed the impact of inflation on the debtor-creditor relationship. An unexpected inflation will redistribute wealth from creditors to debtors because debtors can pay back their debts in dollars of depreciated purchasing power. If both the creditor and the debtor had anticipated the inflation when their loan agreement was contracted, they would have accounted for the inflation. The creditor would have demanded a higher interest rate to compensate for the depreciated purchasing power of the dollars he would be repaid. The debtor would have paid those higher rates willingly.

One of the authors took out an NDEA loan while in college in the sixties. The interest charge was 3 percent. Since then prices have been rising at 3, 4, 5, and even 6 percent a year. What is the true (purchasing power) cost of a 3 percent loan when prices are rising at 6 percent? The cost is −3 percent, a negative real rate of interest. It's too bad we can't get loans like that today.

The nominal rate of interest is the real rate of interest plus the expected rate of price change. The real rate of interest is determined by individuals' desires to save and by the supply of investment opportunities.

When you save, you exchange rights to current consumption for rights to future consumption. Savings represents a demand for future consumption. Saving enables you to consume at an optimal rate. Given your total current wealth, the more current consumption you give up, the more valuable it is in comparison with future consumption. To induce people to save more, they must be offered a higher real rate of interest.

Investment represents the supply of future consumption embodied in some durable good—a machine or a house. All durable goods embody the supply of future consumption in some form. Most durable goods are produced under conditions of increasing costs in the short run; therefore more will be supplied only if the market price goes up. In addition, the increased supply of future consumption may lower the future price of consumption. The larger the quantity of investment, the lower will be the rate of exchange between present consumption sacrificed and future consumption supplied. It will be profitable to produce more durable goods only if the real rate of interest falls. Business investment and housing construction are particularly sensitive to changes in the *real* rate of interest.

The equilibrium real rate of interest produces a desired level of investment which just equals the amount of savings individuals provide at that real rate of interest.

The estimated real rate of interest in the U.S. has fluctuated very narrowly between 3 and 4 percent. It has been amazingly stable. Most changes in nominal rates are due to changes in the expected rate of price change. As you recall, there was very little inflation from 1960 to 1965. Consumer prices rose at 1.2 percent a year. Beginning in 1965 price rises started to accelerate. Inflation continued to rise at ever-increasing rates until inflation peaked at over 6 percent annually in early 1970. People seem to base their expectations of future inflation on recent rates of inflation, for nominal interest rates rose almost in tandem with the rate of inflation. The Corporate Aaa rate was about 4.5 percent in 1965. The previous 5 years had averaged only a 1.2 percent rate of inflation. It seems likely, then, that the real rate of interest was about 3.5 percent. After 3 years of accelerating inflation the corporate Aaa rate peaked at about 8.5 percent in early 1970. Since prices were rising at a rate of 5.5 percent during 1968 and 1969, the interest rate of 8.5 percent makes the real interest rate seem somewhat low in comparison to 1965.

When the distinction is made between real and nominal interest rates, it is not surprising that periods of inflation are associated with high interest rates, Rep. Wright Patman notwithstanding.

# 13

# THE ECONOMICS
# OF HOW YOUR FEDERAL RESERVE
# HAS VIEWED INTEREST RATES

Interest rates have had a key role in policy formulations of both the Federal Reserve and the Treasury. The financial press still interprets interest rate changes as an indication of monetary policy changes. For example, in June of 1971, the *Wall Street Journal* remarked that:

> The Federal Reserve System has maintained its restrictive stance in carrying out monetary policy. . . .
>
> The money managers' restrictive stance was evidenced by a . . . continued upward move in money-market interest rates.

In view of Irving Fisher's 1896 discovery, it is possible that rising nominal interest rates could be viewed as an indication that people expect higher rates of inflation.

Most of the major mistakes made by the Federal Reserve were due to the use of nominal interest rates as indicators of monetary policy. Low or falling market interest rates were interpreted by the Federal Reserve as indicating an expansionary monetary policy, while high or rising interest rates indicated a restrictive monetary policy. The evidence indicates, however, that periods of rapid monetary growth produce high interest rates and periods of slow monetary growth produce low market rates of interest. Periods of rapid monetary growth produce inflation. When the inflation is anticipated by the public, the nominal interest rate rises to compensate creditors for the depreciating purchasing power of the dollar. Increases in the rate of monetary growth tend to lower market rates of interest only in the short run.

Consider an increase in the rate of monetary growth. Initially the supply of money increases more rapidly than the demand for money. The public will attempt to eliminate the excess money balances by spending more than receipts. They can spend these excess money balances either on goods or on financial assets. Some of this increased spending will bid up the price of financial assets and market rates of interest will fall. Assuming that inflationary expectations have not yet changed, this fall in market rates is equivalent to a fall in the real interest rate also. As real rates of interest fall, however, desired expenditures on both consumption and investment goods will increase, creating excess demand for goods and services. If desired investment exceeds desired savings, this implies excess demand for goods and services. The excess demand for goods and services will increase nominal income by producing either an increase in output and/or an increase in prices. The increase in nominal income will increase the demand for money until the excess money balances are eliminated. Once excess money balances are eliminated, the real rate of interest will probably return to its former level.

The higher rate of monetary growth will eventually result in a higher rate of inflation. As the public readjusts their expectations to a higher rate of inflation, the nominal rate of interest will rise until an inflationary premium fully compensates creditors for the higher rate of inflation.

During World War II the Federal Reserve's primary objective was to assure the Treasury funds adequate to meet all government expenditures. In March 1942, the Open Market

Committee asserted its desire to prevent a rise in the interest rates of government bonds during the war. From 1942 until 1951 the Federal Reserve either "pegged" or supported the rate of interest at a very low level: 2.5 percent on long-term bonds, three-eighths of a percent on 90-day Treasury bills. This is one period in which a low interest rate corresponded to expansive monetary policy.

To maintain such a low rate of interest the Federal Reserve had to buy all of the government bonds offered when interest rates started to rise above the support level. Anybody could get cash in exchange for governments. In our discussion of the determinants of the money supply, we explained that every time the Fed bought a bond, reserves increased and there was a multiple expansion of the money supply. The money supply grew 12.1 percent a year from 1939 to 1948 as a result of the Federal Reserve's forced bond purchases. The Federal Reserve had essentially abandoned control over the monetary system during this period of bond support.

After the end of the war, the Fed did not at first unpeg the entire interest structure of the federal debt. Only in 1947 did it request such a change in policy. It wanted to unpeg short-term 90-day rates. When the Treasury agreed to this, the Fed finally got some control over liquidity in the economy. But it was not until the Fed-Treasury Accord of March 4, 1951 that full control over the money supply was given back to the Fed.

However, not until 1970 did monetary aggregates become a chief policy decision variable in the eyes of the Fed. In the January meeting of the Open Market Committee, the members stated their desire to have increased emphasis placed on achieving specific rates of growth of certain monetary aggregates such as the total of currency and demand deposits.

Historically, this change was extremely significant. Up to 1970 a typical directive to the account manager of the Open Market Desk of the New York Fed would read:

> . . . to foster financial conditions conducive to re-
> sistance of inflationary pressures . . . system open

> market operations until the next meeting of the
> Committee shall be conducted with a view to main-
> taining firm conditions in the money market. . . .[1]

"Firm" conditions are associated with high interest rates; "easy" conditions mean low interest rates. Obviously, numerous policy mistakes are possible using the above logic.

Interest rates have been particularly poor indicators of monetary policy since 1967. After 1967 the rate of inflation accelerated from about 3 percent to over 6 percent. Nominal interest rates rose from 5 percent to over 8 percent. This rise in interest rates fooled the Fed and gave them an excuse for what was their mistake. During 1968 to 1969 the Open Market Committee issued directives to the Open Market Desk (like the one above) instructing them to maintain "firm" conditions in the money market. What was "firm" to the Fed were the rising market rates of interest. Chairman William McChesney Martin could tell Congress and the President that the Fed was doing its job in the fight against inflation. Meanwhile critics of the Federal Reserve were pointing out that the money supply was increasing at over 7 percent a year, the fastest rate of growth in the money supply in the postwar period.

Surprising as it may seem, the way to produce "firm" money markets (or high market rates of interest) is to increase the rate of monetary growth. This policy may temporarily reduce interest rates. Soon, however, total spending will rise and this will increase the demand for loanable funds. The rate of inflation will accelerate, and eventually nominal interest rates will reflect expectations of continued inflation. These "firm" money market conditions are the result of "easy" money.

During the summer of 1971 (when this book was written) interest rates and the growth of the money supply were again in the headlines of the financial press. Interest rates rose very rapidly at the same time that the money supply was expanding at phenomenal rates. Critics have accused the Fed of

[1]May 28, 1968 meeting of the FOMC.

switching to a restrictive monetary policy because of the rising interest rates. Those observers watching the growth of the money supply feared that the then current rate of monetary growth was excessive. One can now understand the Nixon administration's confusion concerning monetary policy. By the publication of this book, the Federal Reserve may have reverted to the use of interest rates as indicators of monetary policy.

After that, *le déluge.*

# 14

## THE ECONOMICS
## OF NOT BUYING
## U.S. SAVINGS BONDS

A recent bond drive at the University of Washington was initiated by a general letter from the president of the university to all faculty members. It stated among other things that U.S. Savings Bonds have been responsible for the fiscal stability of our country.

A recent ad in *Newsweek*, presented as a "public service in cooperation with The Department of the Treasury and The Advertising Council," was entitled: "Wouldn't it be a shame if you saved a pile of money for retirement and there was nothing to retire to?"

The ad went on: "There's only one way to save money that insures your country's future at the same time.

"That's U.S. Savings Bonds."

U.S. Savings Bonds aren't new, of course. They are one of ten series of bonds sold by the Treasury to the public since 1935. These Series E bonds can be sold only to individuals. They were a patriotic issue during World War II. There were seven War Loan drives and a concluding Victory Loan, occurring at 5-month intervals from November 1942 to December

1945. They were sold for two reasons: (1) to help finance the war, and (2) to increase savings and hence decrease the inflationary demand created by inflated pay checks.

Buying U.S. Savings Bonds is of course one avenue of savings which, at first glance, contains no risk. That *Newsweek* advertisement even said so: " . . . there is no risk. If your bonds are lost, or burnt, or stolen, we [U.S. government] simply replace them without cost." In addition you are guaranteed that the principal and the interest will be paid to you because they are backed by the taxing power of the United States government. Certainly you could invest in other avenues and obtain higher earnings. Usually, though, higher earnings are associated with higher risk. Securities bought from the U.S. government are by far the safest type of investment one can obtain. A little higher up on the spectrum of risk versus rate of return are corporate bonds. Corporate bonds are now yielding about 6 to 8 percent a year, with call protection for at least 10 years.[1]

Corporate bonds have been known to fail, though, as became painfully obvious with the bankruptcy of the Penn-Central Railroad. Therefore, in order to obtain a higher rate of return one must pay for it in increased risk. At the extreme end of the spectrum of risk and rates of return are located such volatile investments as speculative over-the-counter stocks, penny mining stocks, even long shots at a pari-mutuel horse racing window. High rates of return for your savings can only be obtained by your willingness to accept more risk, that is, higher variability in these rates of return over the life of the investment.

Now look at all of these prospective rates of return in the face of our ongoing inflation. If a Series E U.S. Savings Bond yields you a 5.5 percent rate of return, how much are you really obtaining if there is 6 or 7 percent inflation? The rate of return on U.S. Savings Bonds does not even cover the current loss in the purchasing power of the dollars you are

[1]Call protection insures you that the corporation which issued the bond cannot recall it from you for a specified period of years.

handing over to the government. This is also true for savings accounts which yield only 5 percent. This of course does not mean that you should not save at all.

If you keep all your savings in a checking account, the rate of return you obtain is nominally zero but is really equal to a negative number because of the decrease in the purchasing power of those dollars while they sit in the bank. If you have $100 in your checking account today, and the rate of inflation is 6 percent a year, that $100 will purchase only about $94 worth of goods and services next year, measured in today's dollars. Your real rate of return on any savings which you have invested is equal to the nominal rate paid you minus the rate of inflation.

Even though U.S. Savings Bonds are supposedly risk-free, they do not guarantee that you will have made a good investment. U.S. Savings Bonds (and all other bonds) are fixed in terms of their nominal yield. The 5.5 percent rate of return on savings bonds is fixed as a percentage of the par value of the bond. Other bonds are similar but the issuers usually mail out the interest payments every year. The so-called *coupon rate* of a bond is equal to the guaranteed interest payments each year expressed as a function of the par value of the bond. If you paid a bond dealer $1,000 for a guarantee of getting $50 a year in interest payments forever, then the rate of return on that bond would be 5 percent. Let's assume that you purchased such a bond when there was no inflation and no expectation of inflation. What would happen if all of a sudden prices started to rise 5 percent a year and were expected to continue rising at 5 percent a year forever? What would your real rate of return be then? It would be effectively zero because the interest payments would just compensate you for the loss in the purchasing power of the money invested. If you went to sell the bond, do you think you could now get $1,000 for it? Very few people would be willing to pay you such a high price for obtaining only $50 a year in interest payments. If people required a real rate of return equal to 5 percent they would only be willing to pay you $500 for your bond so that they could obtain a nominal rate of return of 10 percent. When inflation is subtracted out of that 10 percent, the real rate of return just equals 5 percent. Therefore, anytime you have a fixed-interest obligation such as a bond and the general interest rate in the economy rises, for whatever reason, the value of your bond will fall. You will sustain a capital loss. On the other hand, if the general interest rate falls, for whatever reason, you will sustain a capital gain—the value of your bond will rise.

If you think that inflation will continue and you are able to obtain a rate of return in excess of that offered by our government on U.S. Savings Bonds and you still buy U.S. Savings Bonds, you are in effect providing the U.S. government with a gift. This gift is equal to the difference between the rate of interest the government would have to pay on a market loan and the actual interest rate paid to you. In order to obtain the yield on a U.S. Savings Bond you are required to hold it for a period of about 5 years. Right now if you are willing to commit yourself to leaving a similar sum of money in a government insured savings account, you can obtain about 1 to 2 percent higher rate of return. That difference times the amount of money you loan to the government is the size of your gift. That is the price you pay for the joy of giving.

# 15

## THE ECONOMICS
## OF EXPLOITING THE SAVINGS
## AND LOAN SHAREHOLDER

The rates offered by savings banks for your dollars are certainly higher than those offered by the U.S. government for Series E Savings Bonds. However, if it were not for U.S. government regulation, savings (time) account yields would be even higher. This has not always been true, but certainly is today with our 6 percent inflation. The Federal Reserve regulates interest payments via Regulation Q. All interest rates paid by banks which are members of the Federal Reserve System are established under Federal Reserve Regulation Q. During the current period of rising interest rates due to increased inflationary premiums, the ceilings established by Regulation Q have created a large differential between government security yields and those yields offered by member banks. For example in January of 1970, the Regulation Q ceiling rate on savings deposits which did not require any maturity or withdrawal notice by the deposit contract was a full 2.6 percent lower than the yield on 30-day treasury bills. The Regulation Q ceiling rate on 30- to 89-day time deposits was a full 3.57 percent below the 90-day treasury bill rate.

Ceilings at insured nonmember banks are set the same as

those of member banks under Regulation Q by the Federal Deposit Insurance Corporation, which was created during the Depression.[1] As of September 1966, mutual savings banks must observe the same rates that are imposed on federally insured mutual savings banks by the FDIC. Moreover, rates paid at savings and loan associations which are members of the Federal Home Loan Bank Board are also obliged to follow the same regulations and must abide by the control of the FHLBB. The legislation established in September 1966 requires that the Federal Reserve System, the FDIC, and the FHLBB must consult with each other whenever one of them is considering a change in ceiling rates for the banks under their respective control.

The ceiling rate of interest that was established by the Banking Act of 1933 and controlled by the Federal Reserve System on all member bank checking accounts is, of course, zero. It is against the law for any bank to pay interest on its checking accounts.

Interest rate ceilings such as those described above were established with the hope that there would be no "destructive competition" in the banking industry. It was hoped that if no interest rate wars were allowed to occur in the banking industry, there would be less chance of bank failures. However, with the development of federal insurance for all deposits in member banks under the FDIC, the likelihood of widespread bank failures was eliminated.

The effects of Regulation Q have been painfully obvious in the past several years, with market interest rates greatly exceeding ceiling rates. One particularly obvious example concerns the housing industry during the latter part of the 1960s and the early part of this decade. Since ceiling rates for

[1]It has been alleged that the FDIC power to insure new banks has reduced the rate of entry into commercial banking by 60 percent. See Sam Pelzman, "Entry into Commercial Banking," *Journal of Law and Economics*, October 1965.

savings and loan associations were below comparable market interest rates available on securities with similar risks, few savings flowed into savings and loan associations in spite of all the free gifts they offered.[2] Even when these same banks were able to sell mortgage money at a rate of 9 percent, they were unable to obtain people's savings to increase the supply of mortgages because they could only offer 5 percent yields to savers. Had they not been regulated they could have raised the yields they offered savers and obtained more funds to increase the supply of mortgages. Mortgage interest rates would not have risen so high and there would have been more mortgage money around.

Current attempts at regulation of interest rates are sometimes justified by policy makers as a necessary control on bank credit for the purpose of economic stabilization. Regulation Q cannot control total credit in the economy. Funds which leave bank savings deposits because of the rate differential will be channeled to unregulated markets. Although the growth of total credit is probably little affected by Regulation Q, the allocation of credit most certainly is. Funds do not flow into the regulated financial intermediaries such as savings and loan associations and mutual savings banks; they therefore flow into unregulated markets where their borrowers are able to obtain funds more cheaply. All those borrowers who rely on banks or other regulated institutions are forced to pay a higher price or may find that funds are simply unavailable. Those who wish to save are put in a similar situation. People with large amounts of liquid funds who have knowledge of capital markets can receive a high rate of return. On the other hand, those who must rely on regulated institutions to hold and accumulate their savings

---

[2]Effective regulation can cause economic agents specializing in only one endeavor to expand into other areas. Thus, savings and loan associations have on occasion become small appliance distributors.

end up receiving a much lower return than if all banks were free to compete.

Interest rate restrictions on our financial markets impose inequities in our economy. They discriminate against the regulated financial institutions, housing, and small savers. If this were generally realized, monetary authorities might perhaps wish to reevaluate their regulation of interest rates.

# 16
## THE ECONOMICS
## OF DEMANDING MORE MONEY

Individuals desire to hold cash balances because of the services currency and demand deposits yield. We earlier made the simplifying assumption that the amount of cash balances which people desire to hold on average is related positively to the level of nominal income. This relationship was developed many years ago and was called the Cambridge equation of the demand for money. It appeared in the writing of such great Cambridge economists as Alfred Marshall, A. C. Pigou, and, of course, John Maynard Keynes. The Cambridge equation expressing the demand for money as a constant fraction of nominal income is obviously an oversimplification, for it does not include the private cost of holding money balances.

Demand deposits and currency (the narrowly defined money supply) earn no interest. If you hold some portion of your wealth in money balances, you must consider that the services yielded by those money balances are worth the interest you forgo. The market interest rate represents the opportunity cost of renting the services yielded by each dollar of money balances. Consequently, the desired real stock of money should be negatively related to its opportunity cost—the market rate of interest.

If we are to correctly specify the amount of money which people desire to hold, we must include the nominal interest rate as an argument in that function. John Maynard Keynes was principally responsible for modifying the demand for money relationship[1] to include the nominal interest rate effect. If nominal interest rates increase, the costs of holding money balances rise. Hence people's demand for money balances is positively related to their nominal income and negatively related to market (nominal) interest rates.

Disturbances which alter the desired savings and/or the supply of investment opportunities may change the *real* interest rate and, as a result, affect the cost of holding money. Indeed, some of the fluctuations in nominal income *can* be attributed to changes in the real rate of interest that affected the demand for real money balances. For example, consider a rise in real interest rates induced by the financing of new investment opportunities. These new investment opportunities may be the result of an investment tax credit which makes additional investments profitable at the current interest rate. Individuals will desire smaller money balances relative to nominal income at the higher market interest rates because of the increased cost of holding money. Even though the money supply remains constant, the attempt by individuals to reduce their money balances will induce excess demand for goods and services. Nominal income will increase by producing either an increase in output and/or prices.

The modification of the demand for money relationship to include nominal interest rates also helps explain why the rate of inflation overshoots its long-run equilibrium rate in adjusting to a more rapid rate of monetary expansion. The inflation premium incorporated into the nominal interest rate increases the cost of holding money balances, inducing a ten-

[1] Also called the liquidity preference function.
[2] In algebraic terms $M^d = k(i)yp$, where the variable k is negatively related to the nominal interest rate, i.

dency to overshoot the equilibrium rate of inflation during the period of adjustment between two different rates of nominal aggregate demand expansion. For a hypothetical illustration of this "overshoot" effect, assume the following:

1. The demand for money is a positive function of nominal income and a negative function of the nominal interest rate.
2. Wages and prices are perfectly flexible.
3. Real output continues to grow at its equilibrium growth rate of 4 percent per annum.
4. The money supply is initially growing at a 4 percent annual rate, and there is a constant price level.
5. The price level is expected to remain constant, making the nominal interest rate equal to the real interest rate of 4 percent (no inflationary premium).

Suppose the money supply accelerates to a 14 percent annual rate of growth. To maintain the previous 4 percent annual growth of *real* money balances, inflation would have to accelerate to (approximately) 10 percent a year because the rate of growth of *real* money balances is equal to the rate of growth of nominal balances minus the rate of inflation. When the equilibrium inflation of 10 percent per annum is fully anticipated, the nominal interest rate will be 10 percentage points higher to compensate for the depreciation of the purchasing power of money. This increased cost of holding money will induce individuals to desire smaller money balances relative to nominal income; that is, they will spend more. Due to the desire for smaller money balances relative to nominal income, the rate of inflation must overshoot its equilibrium rate of 10 percent per annum during the adjustment period. Therefore, for a while, the rate of inflation will exceed 10 percent a year while individuals reduce their *real* money balances to a new level consistent with the higher cost of holding money.

Some economists have referred to inflation as a "tax" on the services yielded by money balances, since inflation increases the costs of holding money. What are the welfare costs associated with that tax? Remember, in Chapter 4 we analyzed the *welfare costs* resulting from an excise tax on beer. Inflation imposes a similar tax on the services yielded by money balances. The welfare cost arguments are analogous. The private cost of holding money balances is the interest forgone; thus, the private cost increases with the nominal rate of interest. The social cost of holding additional money balances is approximately zero. It costs the government practically nothing to print up additional pieces of paper (dollar bills) to hold in our wallets. If everyone held larger demand deposits at commercial banks, the banks' operating expenses probably would not increase, for these expenses are usually associated with withdrawals and transfers of funds, not higher balances held by depositors. Consequently, at positive nominal interest rates the private costs of holding real money balances exceed the social costs (the resources sacrificed to provide real money balances). This divergence between social and private costs induces individuals to hold fewer real money balances than is socially optimal. Society loses the convenience and services those money balances could have provided at zero social cost. In addition, people will consume resources to create money substitutes. An inflation which increases the private costs of holding money will induce people to spend time and effort reducing those private costs. You will spend an increased portion of your time purchasing and selling financial securities to keep your *real* money balances at that lower level consistent with the higher costs of holding money. In fact you may hire a professional to manage your money balances. All the effort and risk consumes real resources. The resulting reduction of real money balances does not save any resources. Consequently, there is a welfare *loss* to society.

If private costs were equal to the zero social costs, you would hold a quantity of *real money balances* at which a small (marginal) increase in those money balances would yield no additional services to you. This *socially optimum* quantity of real money balances would be held if the nominal rate of interest were zero. The nominal rate of interest would be zero if the expected rate of deflation (falling prices) were equal to the real rate of interest.

If the rate of inflation, or "tax" on cash balances, is very high, as during periods of hyperinflation when prices go up at, say, 15 percent a month, you and everyone else will be induced to use less cash. There will be a *suboptimal* utilization of cash balances. It essentially costs society nothing to print money and create checking accounts. But if it costs you, say, 15 percent a month to keep a dollar bill, then the price of using cash far exceeds the social cost. If we continue with this logic, we see that even when there is no inflation, the price of holding cash is not zero because it can be put in a savings account and thereby earn interest. Therefore some economists have suggested that the government should *pay* everybody who holds cash the equivalent of what that money could earn in a savings account. Then the social cost of creating cash balances—zero—would equal the price paid by the public—zero. (You would just be compensated for what you *could* earn with the money.)

# 17

## THE ECONOMICS
## OF KENNEDY'S 1964 TAX CUT
## AND JOHNSON'S 1968 TAX SURCHARGE

After the Kennedy administration took office and the country started "moving again," economic advisors cautioned the President that unless there was a tax cut, the momentum that was building up would soon die, and the economy would relapse into another recession. For several years, the administration fought hard with Congress to obtain a meaningful tax cut. In 1964 Congress finally enacted a substantial tax reduction. The apparent success of this tax cut was heralded as positive proof of the effectiveness of the "new economics."

In spite of the impressive gains in gross national product thought to be the result of 1964 tax cut, similar evidence for the effectiveness of fiscal policy was not forthcoming after President Johnson and his economic advisors convinced Congress to institute the 1968 tax surcharge to fight inflation. We are all by now well aware of the fact that prices did not stop increasing in 1968 and, in fact, have only recently begun to slow down. Questions were asked as to why a tax cut could be effective but a tax increase could not. A debate in economic circles has ensued. The debate centers on the effectiveness of fiscal policy, or whether or not tax cuts can stimulate aggregate demand.

The debate has broken up into two sides—the monetarists and the fiscal policy Keynesians.

In order to fully understand this debate and the theoretical arguments underlying it, we must present the problem in a manner which distinguishes clearly the different methods available for financing a tax cut. Just as the private sector is faced with a budget constraint and cannot spend more than it can earn, beg, steal, or borrow, so is the government sector. Remember, in Chapter 5 we pointed out that government expenditures must be financed by taxes, borrowing from the public, or increasing the stock of high-powered money. If the government cuts taxes as it did in 1964, the resulting deficit will have to be financed by increasing the stock of high-powered money (printing money) or borrowing from the public. Any increase in the stock of high-powered money will usually create a multiple expansion of the money supply, and this is monetary policy—not just fiscal policy.

During the postwar period, policy makers have considered changes in federal taxes a powerful instrument with which to regulate aggregate demand. The impact of changes in taxes on aggregate demand, however, depends upon the way in which they are financed. If the government deficit resulting from a tax cut is financed by an increase in the stock of high-powered money, the monetarists would agree with fiscal policy Keynesians that aggregate nominal spending on goods and services will increase. If the resulting deficit is financed by borrowing from the private sector, however, the tax cut may have little effect on aggregate demand, for there will be no increase in the money supply (assuming the money supply multiplier remains the same).

Suppose a budget deficit is financed by increasing the stock of high-powered money (monetary base). The money supply will increase by a multiple of the increase in high-powered money. If the money balances demanded by the private sector do not increase, individuals and business firms will attempt to reduce their actual money balances. This attempt will be translated into a desire to increase expenditures on goods and services. Nominal income will increase, thus increasing the demand for money, until the public is satisfied with holding their actual money balances.

Most economists readily accept the proposition that fiscal deficits financed by the creation of money increase nominal spending on goods and services. The current difference between the monetarists' and the fiscal policy Keynesians' approaches to economic stabilization centers on the impact of a tax cut financed by borrowing without an increase in the money supply. The switch from tax to debt finance will increase nominal spending only if it reduces the demand for money. This proposition becomes apparent when the analysis focuses on the aggregate budget constraint of the private, nonbanking sector of the economy.

Consider the budget constraint of an individual or business firm:

Change in money balances = Income
- taxes paid to the government
- purchase of financial assets
- expenditures on goods and services

Aggregating all the budget constraints in the private, nonbanking sector, the budget constraint becomes

Change in money balances = After-tax income
- net purchases of government securities
- expenditures on goods and services

If the private, nonbanking sector desires to increase its money balances, desired expenditures on goods, services, and net additions to the government debt will be less than after-tax income. Conversely, when the private, nonbanking sector wants to decrease its money balances, desired expenditures on goods, services, and net additions to the government debt will exceed after-tax income.

Tax changes will not affect aggregate nominal demand for goods and services if both the demand and supply of money are left unchanged. A tax cut increases after-tax income, but borrowing from the private sector will have to increase in order to finance the deficit without increasing the money supply. If the demand for money remains unchanged, the rise in after-tax income is completely absorbed by the government's increased borrowing.

A switch from tax finance to nonmonetary debt finance will increase aggregate demand only if the demand for money is reduced as a result of the tax cut. The fiscal policy Keynesians argue that the increased government borrowing from the private sector to finance the deficit will increase the market interest rate. Such an increase in the market interest rate would reduce the demand for money, relative to nominal income. As individuals attempt to reduce their money balances relative to their income, aggregate demand for goods and services will increase.

This increase in interest rates is not as obvious as it first appears, however, and certainly is not a forgone conclusion. Interest rates will increase only if individuals consider themselves wealthier as a result of the tax cut. After-tax *income* has obviously increased as a result of the tax cut, but total *wealth* has not, because future tax liabilities implicit in the interest obligations of the increased government debt will lower wealth by an amount equal to the increase in after-tax income. If individuals fully discount their future tax liabilities, the desired savings of the private sector will increase by an amount equal to the increased government borrowing, because increased savings will be necessary to provide future earnings to meet taxes to pay the interest on the additional government debt. Under these conditions, the government could borrow from the private sector to finance the tax cut without increasing interest rates.

Interest rates will rise only if individuals fail to fully

discount future tax liabilities and therefore consider themselves wealthier as a result of the tax cut. If they consider
themselves wealthier, their desired savings will not increase
by an amount equal to the additional government borrowing
and market interest rates will rise. The higher interest rate
will tend to reduce the demand for money, but an opposite
force operates to increase the demand for money at every
nominal interest rate. Consequently, the total impact on the
demand for money, and hence on aggregate demand, is uncer-
tain. As you can see, economic theory does not provide us
with a clear-cut answer to the differences between fiscal
policy Keynesians and the monetarists. Our basic theoretical
framework is consistent with both views. The debate, then,
centers exclusively on empirical questions as to the effects of
fiscal policy actions on interest rates and the impact of these
interest rate changes on the demand for money.

The monetarists' approach does not view tax cuts financed
by borrowing as a significant stimulus to aggregate demand.
They argue that the impact of such a tax cut on interest rates
will probably be small and the demand for money seems to
be fairly insensitive to such small changes in interest rates. In
fact, the wealth effect on the demand for money could
outweigh the interest rate effect, causing the tax cut to
reduce rather than increase aggregate demand.

The subtleties in this debate about the effectiveness of tax
cuts for stimulating aggregate demand have, to be sure, remained totally out of the discussion which is presented in the
popular (and financial) press. It is extremely rare for one to
read about a congressional inquiry as to how the tax cut will
be financed. (The Federal Reserve makes the ultimate decision as to how the deficit is financed.) Once it is realized,
however, that the government faces a budget constraint just
as individuals like us do, a much more meaningful discussion
of fiscal policy can begin.

Kennedy's 1964 tax cut was followed by an acceleration in
the growth of GNP. This episode did not, however, provide a
good experiment to test the hypotheses of the monetarists

and the fiscal policy Keynesians. The tax cut coincided with an acceleration in the rate of monetary growth. The fiscal Keynesians could claim that the acceleration of spending was due to the tax cut; the monetarists agreed because the tax cut was financed by money creation.

The Johnson surtax (tax increase) in 1968 could have been used to reduce the expansion of high-powered money or to reduce the borrowing from the public. (We assume that the tax proceeds were not used to increase government expenditures.) If the increased taxes reduced the expansion of high-powered money, monetarists would have expected the surtax to reduce the growth in total spending. However, if the tax increase simply reduced government borrowing, there would be more funds available to finance private purchases. Although the public's after-tax income had fallen, the income that would have been spent purchasing government bonds could be used to purchase goods and services. Consequently, the monetarists expected the surtax to have little effect on the growth of spending unless it was used to reduce the rate of monetary growth.

The fiscal Keynesians argued that the surtax would reduce total spending even if the rate of monetary growth was not affected. If the government used the increased taxes to reduce borrowing, interest rates would come down, they argued. The fall in interest rates would increase the demand for money. As the public attempted to increase their money balances, total spending would slow.

The effects of the surtax (or rather the lack of them) did tend to somewhat support the monetarists. The rate of monetary growth did not slow as a result of the surtax. Total spending did not slow appreciably; in fact, it slowed much less than policy advocates had forecast. It was especially surprising that interest rates merely paused and then continued their upward climb.

Of course, interest rates were adjusting to higher expected rates of future inflation. Perhaps the surtax did hold interest rates below the level they would have reached in its absence.

The fiscal Keynesians could have simply misjudged the increase in inflationary expectations in their forecasts.

This basic analysis can also be applied to arguments for more accelerated depreciation, larger tax write-offs, and a reinstatement of the investment tax credit. All these policies are essentially tax cuts. These tax cuts create deficits which must be financed either by government borrowing or by money creation. These tax cuts do have another aspect, though. Each of these policies increases the rate of return on new investment. The financing of these new investment opportunities that have become profitable because of, say, an investment tax credit will tend to increase market rates of interest. Consequently, dollar for dollar, tax cuts in these forms will have a stronger upward impact on market rates of interest and will thus reduce the demand for money.

We reiterate, anyone who wishes to rationally analyze fiscal policy changes must fully examine the methods by which they are financed. The way in which the fiscal action is financed will determine its impact on total spending.

# 18
## THE ECONOMICS
## OF TAXES AND INFLATION

An article which appeared in the liberal *New Republic* stated that a reduction in taxes would cause inflation. An article which appeared in the conservative *National Review* the same week stated that an increase in taxes would cause inflation. While these two statements are obviously contradictory, the arguments underlying them seem very plausible at first glance. The author of the *New Republic* article pointed out that a decrease in taxes would give people more spendable income, and therefore they would spend more and cause prices to rise. The author of the *National Review* article stated that an increase in taxes, if applied to both corporate and personal income, would cause inflation because businesses would raise their prices in order to keep their normal profit margin.

Let's first examine the proposition that a tax cut will cause inflation. This statement contains some grain of truth, but it is not properly qualified. It is important to know how the government will adjust to the reduced tax revenue. As you recall, the government has a budget constraint just as we all do. If tax revenues fall, the government must either reduce its expenditures or borrow to finance those expenditures if the money supply is not to be affected. If we assume, as the monetarists do, that individuals in the private sector desire to maintain their present money balances, then we should see them use the increase in after-tax income to purchase financial securities or to spend on goods and services.

How do the budget constraints of the government and individuals mesh in this case? If the government increases its borrowing to finance government spending, after the tax cut individuals in the private sector must purchase those securities. Income available to spend on goods and services falls when the government borrows from the private sector. Government borrowing diverts funds from private borrowers who would have used the borrowed funds to finance expenditures. Consequently, there will be no inflationary increased spending on goods. Desired expenditures by the private sector will not increase, for the increased government borrowing will absorb the increased purchasing power resulting from the tax cut.

What if the government adjusts to the tax cut by reducing its spending? The government will not have to resort to increased borrowing, so the private sector's purchasing power increases by the amount of the tax cut. Again, assuming that members of the private sector desire to maintain their money balances, we will see them spend the increased purchasing power or lend it to someone who will. Private expenditures on goods will rise. Total aggregate demand for goods hasn't changed, however, since the government sector has reduced its expenditures by an amount equal to the rise in private expenditures. Since total expenditures have not changed, a general inflation will not occur.

The only time a tax cut *definitely* will be inflationary is when the resulting deficit is financed by printing money. Not only will the purchasing power of the private sector be increased with no offsetting fall in government expenditures, but individuals will in addition find themselves with excess money balances and will attempt to reduce them. The result is inflation.

Of course, if we, as do fiscal policy Keynesians, relax our assumption that individuals in the private sector will desire to maintain their money balances, the tax cut may affect aggregate spending even though the money supply is left unchanged. Suppose the government adjusts to the reduced tax revenue by increasing its borrowing from the private sector to finance government expenditures. If the private sector desires to save the increase in after-tax income, increased loanable funds will be available to the government without any increase in interest rates. Only if individuals feel they are wealthier as a result of the tax cut will interest rates rise. In that case they will not desire to save all of the increase in after-tax income. Interest rates will rise as the government is forced to bid funds away from private borrowers. The increased interest rates may reduce the demand for money, increasing total spending.

What about the argument in the *National Review*? Will an increase in taxes on corporate income induce corporations to raise prices? The corporation income tax is a tax on net income after all expenses are paid. If total spending remains the same, corporations will charge the same profit-maximizing price whether or not their net profits are taxed. Profits after taxes are maximized whenever profits before taxes are maximized. So long as the corporation income tax is less than 100 percent, corporations will attempt to maximize before-tax profits, and therefore an increase in the rate of taxation on these profits will not change the profit-maximizing price and output combination already existing. This is the short-run argument, though.

In an earlier chapter we discussed the effects of taxing the income from capital in the corporate sector but not in the noncorporate sector. In the long run, an increase in income taxes in the corporate sector will lead to higher prices in the corporate sector *relative* to the noncorporate sector. This is so because capital investment will not flow into the corporate sector at the rate it would have in the absence of the higher corporate income tax. The net rate of return in the corporate sector is lower because of the increased corporate income tax. Since resources will tend to flow into the noncorporate sector where the net rate of return is higher, output of the noncorporate sector will expand more rapidly than the output of the corporate sector. Prices in the corporate sector will rise relative to the noncorporate sector. The process will continue until (on the margin) the after-tax rates of return are equal in both sectors. But this does not imply inflation. An inflation is defined as an over-all rise in prices. Relative prices may change due to an increase in taxes that affect one sector of the economy more severely than another. But the over-all price level cannot be affected, except perhaps in the short run before things are adjusted. In a static situation, as prices rise in the corporate sector because less resources are available due to the lower net rate of return in that sector, increased resources will flow into the noncorporate sector, causing prices to fall. In a dynamic (inflationary) situation, during the transition phase prices will rise relatively faster in the corporate sector and slower in the noncorporate sector than they would have in the absence of the corporate income tax.

We have assumed in this analysis of the effects of an increase in the corporate income tax that total spending on goods and services is unchanged. If the corporate income tax is used to finance government spending that otherwise would have been financed by "printing money," the rate of expansion of the money supply will slow. This of course is *deflationary*, not inflationary, for total spending will be less than it would be with a larger money supply. Even if the money supply is not affected by the corporate income tax, the demand for money may be. The fall in the net rate of return on corporate investment destroys investment opportunities whose financing would have produced a demand for loanable funds. Since fewer loanable funds are demanded by the corporate sector, the market interest rate may fall, increasing the demand for money. Thus, total spending may slow, reducing the rate of inflation. (The monetarist claims this effect will be minor, however, for the demand for money seems to be insensitive to such small changes in interest rates.)

If total spending is not affected by the increased corporate income taxes, they will not produce inflation. Some taxes on corporations do, however, seem to cause prices to rise. Many European countries have expressed dismay at the inflationary consequences of a *value added tax*. This particular type of tax is not very well known in the United States, but it has become quite popular in Europe. Essentially it is a tax on the value which is added to raw material costs by the business. The value added consists primarily of labor costs and the profits of business. For example, if a business buys $1,000 worth of material, supplies, and services from other firms and sells the merchandise it produces for $2,000, the value added is $1,000. Therefore, the total of the value added for all firms in the country must equal the sum of all wages, salaries, rents, interest, and profits. Conceptually, the total of all value added is equal to national income. When the value added tax was instituted in the Netherlands, it was touted in Europe as a "fiscal miracle drug." However, 10 months after the value added tax went into effect, newspaper journalists reported that "it set in motion an inflationary spiral." After other countries in Europe saw this, they postponed their own value added tax.

In order to analyze the effects of a value added tax when nominal aggregate demand is constant, let us assume that a country substitutes a value added tax for a corporate income tax. There is no change in total tax revenue. The corporate income tax does not affect the corporations' profit-maximizing prices, since each corporation continues to maximize its before-tax profits. They continue to produce at the point at which the increase in resource costs necessary to produce additional output is equal to the increase in revenue generated by the sale of additional output. An increase in the corporate income tax rate does not affect *short-run* marginal costs, since the tax is not applied to the costs of production; it is applied only to profits. Since the marginal unit of output generates no additional profits, the corporation pays no taxes on that additional output. The value added tax, however, applies to labor expenses as well as profits. The value added tax increases the marginal cost of producing additional output, since the corporation must now pay a tax on the expenses incurred in expanding output, even if increased profits are not generated by the expansion. The increased short-run marginal costs will induce corporations to raise prices to consumers. In effect, the switch from a corporation income tax to a value added tax will partially shift the tax burden from stockholders in the corporation to customers who now must pay the higher prices. There need be no change in total spending, however, since the reduced corporate income tax rate will provide the increased purchasing power with which the private sector can pay the higher prices charged by corporations.

# 19

## THE ECONOMICS
## OF HOW THE GOVERNMENT OBTAINS
## ITS FAIR(?) SHARE OF OUTPUT

Today federal, state, and local government receipts amount to almost one-third of gross national product. Most of these government revenues come from taxes—income, sales, property, estate, and gift. The revenues of federal, state, and local governments did not always account for such a large percentage of gross national product in the United States. Back in 1929 the percentage of gross national product going to government agencies only amounted to a little more than 10 percent. There has been a dramatic secular rise in this percentage. Tax revenues going to government agencies have in general risen during wartimes and fallen afterward. In spite of some very minor declines in the percentage of GNP going in taxes to the government sector, the trend is upward and there is little evidence that we have reached a peak.

Even though one-third of GNP may seem like a large portion going to federal, state, and local receipts, it is by no means unusual in industrialized countries today. Almost all of the countries in Western Europe have higher taxes than the United States. Sweden is a prime example. More than 45 percent of GNP goes to government revenues. In fact, of all the industrialized countries in the Western World, only Spain and Switzerland have taxes which represent a smaller proportion of GNP than they do in the United States.

Government expenditures in the United States usually represent a larger proportion of GNP than do all of the revenues they receive from taxes, for taxation is not the only way that the government can obtain its fair share of total output. The government has at its disposal three methods of financing its expenditures: taxation, borrowing from the private sector, and printing money.

To understand theoretically how the government obtains its share of output, let us look at an equilibrium situation. To start off we know that receipts from the sale of output become the income of individuals. In equilibrium, desired expenditures on goods and services must equal income. If the government sector of the economy is to acquire some part of total output, it must finance its expenditures in such a manner as to create an effective gap between total income in the economy and desired expenditures on the part of the individuals in the private sector. Essentially, the government is only able to bid away part of total output if it is successful in persuading the private sector not to spend all of its income. The government must create a situation where the income of the private sector is greater than desired expenditures on all goods and services by the private sector. The most obvious method of creating such a gap between income and desired expenditures is to tax the private sector. Government taxation of the private sector is a method of finance that reduces the income available for spending on goods and services by the private sector.

Another way of creating a gap between income and desired expenditures is for the government to borrow from the private sector. When the government borrows from the private sector, the income available to the private sector for expenditure on goods and services is reduced. Neither of these two methods of financing government expenditures need cause a rise in the price level, for if individuals desire to maintain their current level of cash balances, desired expenditures on goods and services will fall by the same amount as government expenditures on goods and services rise, due to the reduction of income in the private sector resulting from either taxation or increases in government borrowing.

Now let us consider the third possible method of government financing. The government could simply print money. Many people do not understand how this can create the necessary gap between income and desired expenditures on goods and services in the private sector. After all, the printing of money does not directly take income available for spending on goods and services away from the private sector and give it to the government as do taxation and government borrowing from the private sector. The fact is that money creation on the part of the government can produce the necessary gap through inflation. Money creation by the government in a full-employment situation will lead to rising prices—inflation. It is not the printing of money per se which creates the necessary gap between income and desired expenditures by the private sector but, rather, the resulting inflation.

To understand this process let's go back to the simplified demand for money relationship which we first started out with in Chapter 6. As prices rise people will wish to increase their *nominal* money balances because their *real* money balances have fallen. Members of the private sector will be induced by the increasing price level to use some of their income to add to their money balances. The inflation reduces the purchasing power of nominal cash balances, and this induces individuals to desire larger nominal cash balances to make up for the reduction in their value. The purchasing power of money depreciates at the rate of inflation. In order for individuals to maintain their real cash balances, they must use part of their income to increase their nominal cash balances. In fact they must add to their cash balances at the same rate as that of the current inflation in order to offset the depreciating purchasing power of the dollars they hold in currency and in their checking accounts.

Money serves as a temporary abode of purchasing power. The services which it can purchase depend on the real value of that money, not the number of dollar bills. In this respect money is a very strange asset. In the aggregate, the total number of dollars in existence does not affect the level of services obtainable from that money stock. If we double the number of dollars in the economy, we do not double the real value of the services of that money stock. As we introduce more money into the system we do not change the purchasing power of the total stock over goods and services; rather, in a full-employment situation, we create an inflation.

As individuals attempt to maintain the real value of their cash balances by adding to their nominal money balances, they create the necessary gap between income and desired expenditures in the private sector. The portion of income used to add to nominal money balances creates the gap necessary to allow the government to bid goods away from the private sector. It is in this sense that inflationary government financing is known as a *tax on money balances*.

The real resources which the government can bid away from the private sector by creating inflation is equal to the rate of inflation times the real money balances which the private sector desires to hold.

In our particular banking system the government does not, however, receive all of the proceeds of this tax on money balances. This would be true only if all of the newly created money were a liability of the government. In our banking system it is not. The commercial banks can also expand their stock of monetary liabilities. We explained this when we discussed the size and determinants of the money supply multiplier. The money supply multiplier exists because of the fractional reserve system which is now in effect in the United States. If the commercial banking system also expands its monetary liabilities, the commercial banks share in the proceeds of the inflationary tax on cash balances. Let's see why.

As the government prints more money it increases the currency and the reserves held at commercial banks. The increased reserves created by the monetary authorities enable the commercial banks to purchase assets from the private sector by expanding their own monetary liabilities. For example, if the monetary authorities create $1 billion in high-powered money, the commercial banking system can acquire a multiple of that amount in interest yielding assets from the private sector because of the fractional reserve system which is in effect. If banks were allowed to pay interest on checking accounts, competition among the individual banks would cause them to offer an interest rate on checking accounts. In such a situation all of the proceeds of the inflationary tax that would otherwise be confiscated by the commercial banks would be returned to the consumers in the form of interest on their demand deposits.

The commercial banking system is not a completely competitive industry, though. In the United States our commercial banking system can be thought of as a regulated monopoly. Entry into the banking business is restricted, and the government fixes the interest rate on demand deposits at zero. In this situation commercial banks are able to confiscate part of the inflationary tax because they represent a partial monopoly. That portion of the inflationary tax redistributes income away from holders of money balances in general to the stockholders of commercial banks.

As an aside, it is interesting to speculate that India's recent nationalization of commercial banks may be a ploy by the Indian government to obtain all of the proceeds from the inflationary tax imposed on individuals in that country. Once the banking system is completely nationalized, all of the proceeds from the tax will go to the national government.

Another way of viewing an inflationary tax on money balances is to think of it as a sales tax or an excise tax. We can then consider the welfare costs due to this tax, as we did in Chapter 4. As with all excise taxes, there is a limit to the degree to which the excise tax may be used to finance government expenditures. There is a limit to the resources that can be acquired by taxing one good. This is not an infinite amount. A prohibitively high excise tax will cause people to demand none of the product in question. That is to say, a sufficiently high tax placed on any good will yield zero tax revenues. This is also true with the inflationary tax on cash balances. At some high rate of inflation people do not add at all to their cash balances. The price of holding cash balances becomes prohibitively high. That is, the nominal interest rate—the opportunity cost of holding cash—is so high as to cause the quantity of cash balances demanded to fall to zero. At that point money no longer serves as a temporary abode of purchasing power. A hyperinflation that gets out of hand ends up in a barter system. A commodity currency comes into operation, allowing people to avoid the tremendously high cost of using cash balances as a temporary abode of purchasing power.

In a full-employment situation money creation is strictly equivalent to taxation. Normal methods of taxation can be supplanted by the government's money creation, which in a full-employment situation will cause an inflation and a tax on people's average cash balances. During an inflation every one of you who adds to his nominal money balances is being taxed by the government. The increase in your nominal money balances every year is proof that you have paid your tax.

# 20
## THE ECONOMICS
## OF MILTON FRIEDMAN
## VS. THE KEYNESIANS(?)

At one point in 1971 President Nixon stated that he was a Keynesian. When one of Vice President Spiro Agnew's aides was questioned as to his boss' economic views, he stated that Agnew had also become a Keynesian. It is not entirely clear what they meant by the term "Keynesian." They were implying that they accept the economic policy framework of John Maynard Keynes. But what specifically distinguishes Keynesian from non-Keynesian economics? Even the economics profession has not clearly defined that distinction.

Professor Harry G. Johnson delivered a major address to the 1970 American Economic Association Meeting entitled "The Keynesian Revolution and the Monetarist Counter-Revolution." This title implies a conflict between Keynesian and monetarist economic theory. The monetarist approach has been developed most thoroughly by Professor Milton Friedman of the University of Chicago. To many economists, however, the monetarist approach to economic theory is not basically inconsistent with the writings of John Maynard Keynes. In fact, Axel Leijonhofvud presented a lecture at the 1966 American Economic Association Meetings contrasting

"Keynesian economics" with the "economics of John Maynard Keynes." Perhaps the soundest statement about Keynesian economics was made by Professor Milton Friedman himself, who told a reporter for *Time* magazine that "in one sense, we are all Keynesians now; in another, no one is a Keynesian any longer."

These labels are nothing more than appeals to a famous and respected figure in economic theory as authority in what is basically a debate about the empirical effects of fiscal policy actions not accompanied by monetary expansion. Until the Great Depression very few economists believed that fiscal policy, alone, could be an effective way to stimulate total spending. Although economists generally accepted the proposition that government spending financed by money creation would increase total spending, they doubted that increased government spending financed by taxing or borrowing would have much effect on total spending. They believed that the financing of government spending by taxing or borrowing would simply "crowd out" (reduce) private expenditures by an amount roughly equal to the increase in government spending.

The apparent ineffectiveness of monetary policy during those gloomy years from 1929 to the start of World War II convinced many young economists and even a few older ones that monetary policy was not a useful tool for stabilization of aggregate output. This interpretation was largely based upon the error of using interest rates as an indicator of monetary policy. As you remember, the Federal Reserve has a habit of judging the effects of its monetary policy by market rates of interest. The low interest rates during the thirties, which were a result of expectations of falling prices and a collapse of investment opportunities, were regarded by the Fed as proof of their efforts to stimulate the economy through "easy" money. This mistaken use of interest rates as indicators of monetary policy misled economists into concluding that monetary policy was ineffective.

Actually there was a violent *contraction* of the money

supply from 1929 to 1933 (when the money supply fell by over 30 percent), and recovery may have been halted by an additional contraction of the money supply in 1937. At the time, however, money supply statistics were not readily available. It was not until the early 1950s that the Federal Reserve started collecting accurate figures on the nation's total supply of currency and demand deposits. Current statistical data gathering techniques still do not yield very accurate figures on the money supply in the U.S. The Federal Reserve has been forced to change their money supply time series data at least three times in the past 3 years. The tragic misjudgment of monetary policy in the thirties points up the importance of collecting accurate statistics on the money aggregates.

Into this atmosphere of doubt concerning the ability of monetary policy to stimulate growth in total spending came *The General Theory of Employment, Interest, and Money* (1936) by John Maynard Keynes. In brief, Keynes demonstrated theoretically that fiscal policy could be used as an alternative to monetary policy to stimulate total spending. Keynes' novelty was the idea that people would desire to hold fewer money balances at higher market rates of interest. He called this demand for money relationship the *liquidity preference function*. As we have seen in Chapters 16 and 17, an increase in the rate of interest could affect total spending by reducing the demand for money. As individuals attempt to reduce their cash balances, total spending will increase. Our modified demand for money function presented throughout is of the Keynesian liquidity preference type.

Keynes saw the Depression as a collapse of investment opportunities leading to a low real rate of interest. The demand for money would increase as the real interest rate fell, causing a drop in total spending. Keynes neglected to mention that falling prices created by unemployment would have an effect on expectations of future prices, contributing to a fall in the nominal rate of interest. When aggregate spending fell (in a world of *rigid wages*), the resulting unemployment would destroy new investment opportunities. If the real rate of interest fell dangerously close to zero in a world of falling prices, money balances would bring a higher rate of return than any other asset in the economy. If the nominal rate of interest fell to extremely low levels, perhaps everyone would hold his wealth in the form of money balances, for the opportunity cost of holding money balances would be low. If the monetary authorities increased the money supply by purchasing bonds in open market operations, the seller would not use his increased money balances to buy bonds or other assets. He would merely replace his bond holdings with increased money balances. Although the money supply would increase, so would the demand for money. If everyone remained satisfied with these increased money balances, total spending would not increase. In this so-called *liquidity trap*, monetary policy could not work.

Of course few economists take the *liquidity trap* as seriously now. What has survived from Keynes' *General Theory*, however, is the general specification of the *liquidity preference function*. Stabilization policy shifted from the Fed to the President and Congress. It was generally accepted that the fiscal policy instruments of the Treasury could be used to influence the demand for money instead of concentrating stabilization policies in the Federal Reserve's control over the supply of money.

Fiscal policy works indirectly through the financial markets in changing the interest rate and the cost of holding money. The Keynesian principle of deficit spending is to increase the demand for loanable funds. If the government borrows from the private sector and uses the funds to lower taxes or finance increased government spending, interest rates should increase. The rise in the interest rate would induce individuals to hold fewer money balances relative to their nominal income, increasing total spending.

Of course, some tax cuts will have decidedly more impact on the demand for money than others. An investment tax credit or accelerated depreciation allowance not only reduces taxes but also increases the rate of return on a number of new investment projects. The financing of these new investment opportunities will create an additional source of demand for loanable funds, pushing interest rates up even farther. Even though the investment tax credit and accelerated depreciation give more bang (in the form of increased total spending) for the buck (the loss of tax revenue), they are discriminatory. In contrast to a general tax cut, the major beneficiaries of the investment tax credit will be stockholders in rapidly growing corporations. The major beneficiaries of the increased spending will be manufacturers of producer durables. Other sectors such as housing construction will probably suffer.

In the past decade or so there has been a revival of pre-Keynesian thinking about the significance of the impact of pure fiscal actions on total spending. This is the "monetarist counter-revolution" referred to by Professor Harry G. Johnson. The monetarists believe that fiscal policy actions that are not accompanied by changes in the money supply will have little impact on total spending. The demand for money, they argue, is relatively insensitive to small changes in the rate of interest. Although they do not deny that rising interest rates reduce the demand for money, they regard the effect as a minor one. Moreover, they see fiscal policy actions as having relatively minor effects on real interest rates. Changes in expectations of inflation cause far greater fluctuations in the nominal rate of interest than are likely to be generated by fiscal actions.

Some fiscal actions have greater impact on market rates of interest than others. For example, if the government borrows and then uses the funds to reduce personal income taxes, interest rates may not be significantly affected. The tax savings might be entirely saved. In this case the increased desired savings could just finance the government borrowing with no change in the interest rate. Similarly a tax increase coupled with a decrease in government borrowing may have little effect on the interest rate because the private sector will tend to finance the tax increase with the funds they would have saved. The government's decreased borrowing is matched by a reduction in the supply of loanable funds, leaving interest rates again unchanged. This may be one reason the 1968 surtax did not seem to lower interest rates very much. Changes in the personal income tax produce offsetting movements in private savings because individuals tend to maintain a stable rate of consumption.

The actual response of interest rates to fiscal actions depends upon their impact on consumption expenditures. Consumption expenditures usually depend upon an individual's long-run expectations of future income possibilities that change very slowly. Changes in after-tax income, *especially when announced as temporary*, may have only small effects on consumption expenditures. If taxes go up, an individual can maintain his consumption expenditures only by decreasing his saving. A tax reduction must be saved if it is not to increase consumption expenditures. Increased borrowing to finance additional government expenditures will raise market interest rates, however. Private savings forthcoming at the current market rate of interest will not increase if there are no tax reductions. The government borrowing must compete with private investment opportunities for a limited amount of loanable funds, so interest rates must rise.

Even if such fiscal actions do affect the real rate of interest, they will not have much impact on total spending if the demand for money is insensitive to small changes in market rates of interest, as the monetarists claim. The main effect of rising interest rates will be the reduction of private investment undertaken. Some loanable funds previously used for private investment spending will flow to the government. The higher rate of interest will also reduce desired consumption expenditures. Consequently, the increased government borrowing will merely reduce the income available for spending by the private sector. This is the so-called crowding out effect, in which the financing of government expenditures merely reduces spending by the private sector.

Whatever the fine points of stabilization policy, the government is politically committed to preventing periods of excessive unemployment. This commitment started during the Depression, when at one time 25 percent of the work force was unemployed. Congress and the President were impressed enough by this high rate of unemployment to institute the whole package of New Deal legislation discussed in Chapter 9. Our entry into World War II and concurrent increases in employment assuaged people's fears for the time being. After the war, however, Congress remembered how things could be, and the Full Employment Act of 1946 was passed. It established a federal commitment to be continually responsible for full employment. It was feared that there would be an unemployment problem during the reconversion from a wartime to a peacetime economy. Many senators and congressmen proposed legislation which was reminiscent of the New Deal. The bill which finally passed both the Senate and the House was a compromise measure. The Full Employment Act simply stated that it was the responsibility of the federal government to maintain full employment. The machinery for carrying out this goal was left to the Council of Economic Advisors and the Joint Committee on the Economic Report. They were held responsible for recommending any action the economic situation might warrant.

The President and Congress can effectively carry out suggestions by the Council of Economic Advisors in the realm of fiscal policy. For example, Congress can pass legislation which alters the amount of government spending or the tax structure of the economy (as it did in 1964 and 1968). The executive and legislative branches of the government have control over the budget deficit. However, neither the President nor the Congress has the power to determine how the deficit will be financed. That power lies with the Federal Reserve monetary policy. Congress and the President determine the deficit; the Federal Reserve determines the method which is used to finance the deficit: borrowing from the private sector or increasing the stock of high-powered money.

(Remember that any increase in the stock of high-powered money will create a multiple expansion of the money supply.) Since the Federal Reserve is independent of the President and Congress (although ultimately Congress has control of the Fed since they could amend the act creating the Fed), some observers have maintained that the Open Market Committee of the Federal Reserve System is the most powerful group of 12 men in the world. While readers may not agree with such an inflated view of the members of the FOMC, the fact that they have ultimate control over how the federal deficit is financed gives them the power to offset any stabilization policies agreed on by the President and Congress.

# 21
## THE ECONOMICS
## OF MORTGAGING
## THE FUTURE

Every year it seems that Congress is forced to reconsider the ceiling on our national debt. In 1969 they had to raise it from $358 billion to $365 billion. In 1970 they had to raise it to $400 billion. And in 1971 they had to raise it again. Many people are wondering how the nation can forever remain in debt. After all, it's usually quite difficult for an individual to always operate in the red. Not so for the government, though.

Our national debt was only $1.2 billion in 1902. It has typically risen during wartimes as the government has required larger amounts of financing to cover its tremendous rise in expenditures. Our national debt grew from $1.3 billion before the First World War to $23.8 billion after it. During the Second World War it increased about 500 percent. On the other hand, if we look at the national debt in terms of per capita figures, it has been secularly declining. The per capita national debt was $1,625 in 1940, and today it is about $1,400.

The concern over the national debt arises because of the fact that many people feel that we are imposing a burden on future generations. Every time the government increases its sales of government bonds, future generations are being forced to pay the interest on these contractual arrangements made by the government. To clarify the issue, we first must concern ourselves with only the *net* national debt. The net national debt is the total gross public debt outstanding minus all intergovernmental agency borrowings. For example, if the Treasury issues bonds for $1 million and the Fed purchases $1 million of government bonds in open market operations, the gross public debt will rise by $ 1 million; however, the net public debt will remain constant. We should not concern ourselves with interagency borrowings because they do not affect the future tax liabilities of individuals in the economy.

In order to fully understand the so-called burden of the net public debt, we have to examine two situations. The first one involves making a choice between debt financing of government expenditures and tax financing of those same government expenditures. The second one involves debt financing of government expenditures versus money creation as a method of financing those same government expenditures.

When the government switches from taxation to issuance of debt in order to finance expenditures, future generations will be forced to pay higher taxes in order to pay the interest on this increased government debt. Now, if people today fully anticipate the future tax liabilities inherent in the increased public debt, they will save an amount which will provide them sufficient earnings to maintain their future consumption in the face of higher future taxes. This savings will be equal to the alternative tax. The increased savings will permit private investment to remain at the same level in spite of the increased government borrowing. There will be no increased consumption by current generations at the expense of consumption by future generations; that is, the capital stock in the country will be the same whether or not the government expenditures are financed by increasing the public debt or by increasing taxes. If we measure the burden on future generations as the degree to which their wealth position is lower because of the particular method of financing, then they will suffer no burden if increased government debt is fully understood by the public.

On the other hand, if the future increased tax liabilities inherent in the new government debt are not fully anticipated by this generation, future generations may be worse off; they may suffer a burden. The reasoning is as follows: if people do not fully anticipate the future tax liabilities inherent in the increased public debt, they will feel wealthier. They will therefore increase their present consumption. They will be passing on less real wealth to future generations because they will be consuming more in the present and saving less. Therefore, future generations will inherit a smaller capital stock from the present generation. Future generations will, in some sense, be burdened by not having as large a capital stock as otherwise would exist.

Members of the present generation *voluntarily* decide to buy government debt; that is, on the margin the interest rate paid them by the government for sacrificing current consumption today is just enough to make them indifferent between consuming today and waiting to consume in the future when they are paid back the principal of the government debt. On the other hand, members of future generations will be forced involuntarily to pay higher taxes in order to pay back the interest on the increased government debt. If the public feels that they can pass some of the burden of taxes on to the next generation, they will feel wealthier as a result of financing government spending by borrowing.

What would happen if the increased government expenditures were financed by printing money? Money creation results in inflation in a full-employment situation. Inflation creates the necessary gap between income and desired expenditures on the part of the public so that the government may bid away resources from the private sector. People are being taxed on their cash balances. If people wish to maintain a certain fraction of their nominal income in cash balances, they will be forced to add to their cash balances at the rate of inflation. That is, in order to maintain the real value of their cash balances, people must make up for the depreciation in their cash balances due to inflation by adding to them at the same rate as inflation. Of course, as we discussed earlier, this tax on money increases the cost of holding money. Individuals will desire to hold smaller real money balances. The increased cost of holding money will induce individuals to demand more money substitutes. Some economists claim that individuals will desire to save more and consume less because financial assets are substitutes for money as a means of maintaining a stock of liquid purchasing power. Thus, inflationary finance may increase the real wealth of future generations because of the increased savings it generates.

If there are unemployed workers at current wage rates, and wages are not flexible downward for some reason (perhaps expectations change very slowly), the expansion of monetary and nonmonetary debt may increase the total stock of wealth handed down to the next generation. As mentioned above, in a full-employment context all the resources used to produce goods for the government must be bid away from private wealth-producing uses. Suppose, however, there are unemployed resources (especially labor). If government expenditures are financed in such a way as to increase total spending and employment, the government may use resources which otherwise would have been unemployed. The total stock of wealth will have increased for both the current and future generations because wealth has been created without diverting resources away from other wealth-producing uses. Since the use of monetary finance will probably stimulate total spending the most, it might be preferred in unemployment situations by both current and future generations.

In all of the above cases we have ignored completely the possibility of borrowing from other countries. We have only considered the situation where debt expansion involved the private members of our own economy. Actually, foreigners

own about 5 percent of our national debt. In a full-employment situation, if the government chooses to obtain resources
from other countries by increasing the public debt, future
generations will, to be sure, be saddled with higher taxes to
pay foreigners the interest and principal on the loans they
have given us. Sometime in the future those resources must
be paid back through a trade surplus—that is, part of our
future output will not be available for domestic use because
exports will have to exceed imports. Future generations are
not, however, necessarily worse off. Future generations will
enjoy a higher capital stock because of the resources that
were borrowed from foreign countries during full employment in our own country. Given our rate of consumption, we
could not have increased our own capital stock without going
to other countries in such situations. If the government
expenditures had been borrowed from the private sector,
those funds would have had to be taken out of private
wealth-producing uses. If the yield on the increased capital
stock made available by resources borrowed from other countries exceeds the interest payments on the increased public
debt sold to foreigners, then future generations will be better
off.

# 22

# THE ECONOMICS
# OF BUYING A VOLKSWAGEN
# INSTEAD OF A FORD

It's relatively ugly. It's relatively slow. It's relatively unstable. It's relatively cramped inside. Nonetheless, there are hundreds of thousands of happy Volkswagen owners in the United States. Why have so many people decided to buy the Beetle instead of, for example, a Ford or a Chevy or an AMC car? Any of you readers who have purchased a Volkswagen know the reason—it's cheaper than an American car. Americans buy foreign cars when they think they are getting a better deal by doing so. This is of course true in all voluntary transactions. People will only trade when there are gains to be made in the process; that is, people will only transact business with other people voluntarily if both parties feel that they are made better off by the transaction. In the international economic sphere, the same is true. Nations will trade among themselves because there are gains to be had from such trading.

The amount of world trade has increased dramatically in the last 172 years. In 1800 it was a mere $1.36 billion in terms of current purchasing power. Just before the Depression, it had reached almost $70 billion. The Great Depression slowed things down a bit, and that figure was not to be reached again until 1950. Today world trade averages in excess of $300 billion a year. If countries did not realize that they were all gaining from this increased world trade, it would not be growing at such a fast rate. After all, the transactions involved are, for the most part, voluntary, between individual citizens in different countries. Even though the argument in favor of world trade is a relatively simple one, it is difficult for some unions and industries to accept the declines in demand for their services or products that may come about as a result of increased world trade.

In order to understand why all nations can be made better off as a result of trade, we must distinguish between a nation's *comparative* advantage in the production of a good or service and a nation's *absolute* advantage in producing a wide variety of goods. The United States may have an absolute advantage in producing a wide variety of goods in the sense that it can produce those goods with fewer man-hours of labor. This does not mean that the United States will not trade with other countries. On the contrary, the United States benefits by specializing in only those endeavors in which it has a comparative advantage. An example of comparative advantage may clarify this statement.

William Howard Taft was perhaps the best stenographer in the world before he became President. He had an absolute advantage in stenography. When he became President, by definition, he also had an absolute advantage in being President. As President, he did not specialize in stenography even though he was the best. The advantage to him and to the nation of devoting all his time to being President was much greater than the loss of his stenographic output. His comparative advantage lay in presiding over the nation, not in taking dictation at 200 words per minute.

The United States may have an absolute advantage in the production of computers and roller skates, in the sense that we can produce both goods with fewer man-hours of labor than anyone else. However, we let other countries produce roller skates for us because our comparative advantage lies in producing computers. We gain from exchanging the computers we produce for the roller skates produced by other countries.

In general, people discover their own comparative advantage by contrasting the return from doing one job with the return from another one. An executive in a large corporation may have an absolute advantage in doing 15 different tasks for that company. For example, he may be able to type better than all of the secretaries, wash windows better than any of the window washers, file better than any of the file clerks, and carry messages better than any of the messengers. His comparative advantage, however, lies in being an executive. He knows that his comparative advantage lies in this job because he is paid more for being an executive than he would be paid in any of those other jobs. The company willingly pays his salary as an executive because the value of his output in that job is at least as large as the salary paid him.

The key to understanding comparative advantage lies in the realization that total resources are fixed at any moment in time. An individual, a company, or a nation must decide how it will allocate its available resources at a given moment. No one can use a resource in two different jobs at the same time. Even if companies or nations are absolutely better at doing everything, they will still specialize in those tasks in which they have a comparative advantage, for in that specialization they maximize the return from the use of their time and resources.

Japan is a good example of how a nation can benefit from exploiting its comparative advantage and engaging in a large volume of world trade. Japan's recovery since World War II has been as miraculous as was Germany's. Real income in that country has been growing at an average rate of about 10 percent a year. Foreign trade has grown at an even faster rate. While real income doubled between 1952 and 1960, for example, exports from Japan more than tripled. During the early sixties Japan's exports were doubling almost every 5 years. Japan has used its comparative advantage in manufacturing to expand its export markets in cameras, automobiles, and, believe it or not, steel products. It is hard to imagine how a country without a resource base composed of the raw materials needed to make steel products can become a net exporter of them, but Japan's comparative advantage is in the machining of the steel and not in the exploitation of raw resources to make it; therefore, Japan imports iron ore and exports cold rolled steel.

Many American producers are fighting to restrict Japanese imports into the United States. Some industrial spokesmen claim that Japan has an absolute advantage (in the sense of man-hours consumed to produce a good) in some areas. Even in those areas in which Japan must consume more man-hours to produce goods than the United States, the lower wage rates paid in Japan may still permit producers there to undercut the prices of American producers. These are problems of exchange rate adjustment which we shall discuss in later chapters. Exchange rates must reflect the differences in purchasing power of the different currencies to insure that the value of exports from one country is matched by an equal value of imports from other countries. When exchange rates are free to adjust to account for the differences in purchasing power among currencies, each country will produce only those goods in which it has a comparative advantage. It may turn out that the Japanese will have a comparative advantage in producing automobiles. The American automobile companies fear that this may be happening. This is why Ford, General Motors, Chrysler, and American Motors are screaming for help.

# 23

## THE ECONOMICS
## OF HELPING FORD MOTOR
## COMPANY AND UNITED STATES STEEL

As Japanese-made Toyotas, Datsuns, and Mazdas have consistently increased their sales in the United States, American automobile producers have started to feel the pinch. Recently, an executive of Ford Motor Company requested that the administration push for restrictions on the imports of foreign automobiles into the United States. Even more recently, the Chairman of United States Steel, Edwin Gott, stated that our country's attempt to increase foreign trade was "woefully out of touch with the times." Mr. Gott and many other steel executives want much tighter controls on steel imports. They want these controls to spell out not only total tonnage to be admitted but also the amounts of each particular type and the places to which the steel can be shipped.

More than two centuries ago the mercantilists had similar ideas about what was good for the nation. They felt that it was proper for a country to expand its exports without expanding its imports in order to acquire large amounts of gold; that is, they felt that a trade surplus was the only way a nation could gain from trade. This idea is expressed by modern-day patriots who feel that "if I buy a Nikon from

Japan, I have the camera and Japan has the money. On the other hand, if I buy a Kodak in the United States, I have the camera and the United States has the money."

Of course this notion ignores the concept of comparative advantage developed in the last chapter. In the long run, exports have to equal imports. Countries do not ship goods to other countries and get nothing but pieces of paper in return; they will trade goods only for other goods.

Because nations, including ours, have at times felt very strongly about limiting cheap exports from foreign countries, we have had periods of very severe tariffs in the United States. A tariff is a tax on commodities which are imported into our country. The first U.S. tariffs were imposed in 1816 as a protective measure against British imports. These tariffs were to be the model for the tariffs of 1824, 1828, 1832-33, 1842, 1846, and 1857.

In 1861 the Morill Act started a long series of legislation which raised tariffs in order to help finance the Civil War. By 1864 tariffs were up to 47 percent. In 1890 the McKinley Tariff increased the average rate even higher, up to 50 percent. Tariffs went down to about 25 percent in 1913 with the passing of the Underwood-Simmons Bill. Tariffs continued to fluctuate up and down, reaching their highest level in 1930 with the passage of the Smoot-Hawley Tariff. Today average tariff rates are about 10 to 15 percent.

The effects of import tariffs on the over-all welfare of our economy can be analyzed in a manner similar to that in which we analyzed the effects of sales taxes on specific commodities. We refer to the general welfare cost analysis which we gave in Chapter 4. We warn the reader that, as always, this welfare cost analysis does not distinguish between who gains and who loses, in the sense that no special weight is attached to the gains or losses of one individual as opposed to another.

Let's consider the situation in which steel is produced in the United States and also imported into the United States. Suppose that the United States can purchase all the steel it wants, in the absence of tariffs, at the going world price of steel. U.S. producers are not technologically efficient enough to produce all the steel Americans demand at the currently prevailing world price. American producers can be induced to furnish more domestically produced steel only through an increase in the domestic price of steel. In the face of world competition, this is impossible without tariffs.

Now suppose that Congress places a tariff on imported steel. The domestic price of steel can increase above the world price of steel, for anyone in the United States who wishes to purchase foreign steel must pay the before-tax world price plus the tariff. The government obtains revenue from all the imports of steel into the U.S. Now that the effective world price of steel is raised in the domestic economy, U.S. producers of steel can profitably expand their production. They will have to bid resources away from other sectors of the economy, though. The increased production of steel necessitates a reduction of production somewhere else in the economy. Of course, now that domestic production of steel has increased, we will import less. Some resources were used in export producing sectors of the economy to produce the exports needed to exchange for imported steel. Since the imports of steel have been reduced, those resources used in producing exports to exchange for the imports are released to produce other goods. The fact remains, however, that our given stock of resources will yield less steel by reallocating its production to the domestic steel industry. We could have acquired more steel with the same resources if we had left resources in the export producing sector and traded those exports for foreign steel. This is so because of America's *comparative advantage* in the production of the export goods.

What about the consumers of steel? When the domestic price of steel rises, less will be demanded by consumers. Manufacturers will use less steel and more substitutes for steel. They have an incentive at the higher domestic price of steel to develop production techniques which minimize the use of steel. As consumers of steel switch to substitutes which are produced domestically, some resources used to produce the exports needed to trade for imported steel will be released from those export industries. These resources can now be used to produce steel substitutes. However the value of these steel substitutes produced will necessarily be less than the value of the imported steel those exports could have been traded for. If not, the resources would already have been used in steel substitute production. The resources were in the export industry to begin with because they had a comparative advantage in the production of exports.

The payment of the tariff on the remaining imports of steel reduces the consumer surplus of steel consumers but this is not a part of the welfare loss, for the tax revenue can be returned to society in the form of a tax cut elsewhere.

Import tariffs, therefore, create welfare losses just like any other taxation of specific products. The United States gets less from the use of its resources because the resources shift out of, say, export industries and into domestic production of steel or steel substitutes and thus are no longer being used in the areas in which they have a comparative advantage. People are faced with a set of prices that no longer reflects the social (world) costs of production. Consumers will purchase less steel than is socially optimal and producers in the U.S. will produce more steel than is socially optimal.

There are, however, certain situations in which some tariff may be optimal. Remember in the above analysis we assumed that the U.S. could buy as much steel as it wanted at the going world price. If the United States purchases a very large proportion of the world's output of some good, say coffee, the United States may be better off if it imposes an import tariff on coffee. Every time consumers in the United States collectively desire to increase their consumption of coffee, they must be willing to pay a higher price to elicit an increased supply from the world market. That means that the social cost to Americans of purchasing more coffee is the cost of the additional coffee purchased plus the increment in price paid on the preexisting level of coffee purchases. Each individual consumer will ignore that last term since he, individually, has no effect on the price of coffee. The cost of an additional unit of coffee to one individual is less than the cost of that additional unit of coffee if all American consumers simultaneously increase their consumption. If a tariff is placed on imported coffee, the amount of coffee demanded by Americans will be reduced. This reduction in the demand for coffee will cause the world price of coffee to fall. At the lower world price, it costs the United States fewer exports to purchase each unit of imported coffee, creating a gain in consumer surplus that was not accounted for in the previous analysis of the welfare losses resulting from tariffs. In order to make the amount of coffee demanded in the United States consistent with the actual marginal cost to the United States of buying additional coffee, the American government could put an import tariff on coffee which would make the private cost to each consumer equal to the social cost to the United States. Unless the tariff is placed on imports of coffee, all individual coffee drinkers in the United States will together consume more than what is socially optimal from the United States' point of view. The world price of coffee will be higher, and the United States will have to export more to pay for every cup of coffee.

The situation is reversed when the country has a monopoly on the export of a good. Brazil, for example, supplies a very large proportion of the world's coffee. Although each individual producer of coffee in Brazil has little impact on the price of coffee, all Brazilian producers taken together do have an important effect on the price of coffee. Each producer regards the increase in revenue generated by selling one additional unit to be the going world price for that unit. If, however, all the producers simultaneously increase their production of coffee by one unit, the world price will fall. If all producers simultaneously increase output, marginal revenue to each producer will be the new world price minus the loss sustained from selling all previous output at a lower price.

Thus competition will force producers to produce too much and will drive the world price down. In this situation the Brazilian government can institute an optimal tax on the exports of coffee so that production of coffee will decrease until marginal cost equals (social) marginal revenue. Social marginal revenue accounts for changes in the world price induced by the simultaneous expansion or contraction of output by all producers; private marginal revenue, as it appears to each individual producer, does not. With the optimum tax on coffee exports, output will be lower than the free trade level, but the world price of coffee will be higher. Brazil can get more imports for each unit of coffee exported.

These arguments for the optimum tariff or export tax assume that no other country will retaliate by increasing tariffs on imports or export taxes. If, for instance, the U.S. puts a tariff on coffee imports and Brazil puts a tax on coffee exports, both countries could be worse off. Once other countries can retaliate by placing trade restricting taxes on their imports or exports, the free trade situation may be the optimum solution even if a country has significant monopsony power over imports or monopoly power over the products exported.

One interesting postwar development in international trade policies has been the emergence of tariff unions. Europe has instituted a tariff union on a very large scale. In 1955, six European countries agreed to form the European Economic Community. In March of 1957 the Treaty of Rome was signed by Germany, France, Italy, the Netherlands, Belgium, and Luxembourg. Tariffs among the members of the Common Market were immediately reduced. It was hoped that by 1969 all tariffs would be done away with and a uniform tariff against nonmember imports would be instituted. Although the historical record has not been this impressive, much has been accomplished since 1957. By July of 1963, all quantitative restrictions on trade between members were abolished, and tariffs were cut to 60 percent of their 1957 level. By 1968, a uniform tariff was erected against outside imports.

The effects on total trade within the Common Market have been rather impressive. Between 1958 and 1967, trade increased at a rate of $2 billion a year. Nonmember nations have looked on with envy at the benefits from freer trade within the Common Market. As is well known, England has repeatedly attempted to enter the EEC. It was not until many months after Charles de Gaulle's death that members of the Common Market finally agreed to permit England's entry. The United States sees the expansion of the Common Market as a threat to its leadership in world trade, as it well should. Common Market members have consistently attempted to discriminate not only against the United States, but against all nonmembers.

In the United States, President Kennedy attempted to obtain lower tariffs. In October 1962 Congress gave him the authority to negotiate reduction of tariffs by passing the Trade Expansion Act. This act was meant to allow the United States to increase its negotiating ability in international trade conferences. In the past, this ability had been seriously hamstrung by the lack of administrative authority in matters of tariffs. The Trade Expansion Act sought to allow the United States to multilaterally cut tariffs by 50 percent. The Common Market had constructed high tariffs against the United States trade. The Trade Expansion Act sought to ameliorate this situation.

In the Spring of 1962, a conference under the General Agreement on Trade and Tariffs (GATT) was convened to discuss tariff reduction. This conference came to be known as the Kennedy Round. Over 600 delegates from 82 countries were present. However, it wasn't until June of 1967 that any agreement was actually reached in the Kennedy Round. As can be expected, during the Kennedy Round Conferences, the big disagreements centered on the size and nature of the tariff cuts. The U.S. wanted to have equally large reductions on all tariffs. The Common Market countries wanted to reduce some tariffs more than others and some not at all. A compromise measure full of diplomatic loopholes was finally adopted.

The Kennedy Round Conference in 1963 was the sixth such conference held under the auspices of GATT since the end of World War II. It lasted longer and accomplished more than any other similar conference. The final agreement of the Kennedy Trade Round subjected $40 billion of trade to new tariff policies. Agricultural products especially faced substantially lower tariffs as a result of the Kennedy Round.

As prices in the U.S. have risen faster than in other countries, American manufacturers have asked not for more reductions in tariffs, but, rather, for increases in tariffs. It is thought that the present system allows other countries to encourage their exports with special tax rebates, allows growing regional groups to do business tariff-free among themselves, and allows Japan to keep quota limits against numerous U.S. items while flooding the United States with Nikons, Toyotas, and cheap synthetic textiles. The U.S. is now striking out at supposedly unfair imports ranging from Japanese glass to French molasses. It was reported that at GATT headquarters in Switzerland an aide described the Nixon administration's attitude as "fantastically dangerous" for the future of liberal trade in the world.

The fact is that in 1971, for the first time in 20 years, the U.S. suffered a deficit in its trade balance for 3 months in a row. In the next chapter we shall examine why imports into the United States are exceeding exports to the rest of the world.

# 24
## THE ECONOMICS
## OF LETTING THE
## DOLLAR FLOAT

TREASURY OFFICIAL SAYS
"DRAMATIC" STEPS WON'T SOLVE
WORLD'S MONETARY PROBLEMS

U.S. HAD DEFICIT IN TRADE IN MAY,
SECOND MONTH IN ROW

REP. REUSS WOULD LET
DOLLAR FLOAT DOWN

The above are headlines from various newspaper articles last year that were concerned with the international monetary crisis. Other countries have been finding themselves with increasing supplies of U.S. dollars. Little more than a decade ago, the headlines were just the reverse; they talked about the dollar shortage problem—the shortage of dollars for world trade and the possibility of that trade drying up if international liquidity wasn't increased. To understand the origins of the current international monetary problems, we must go back in history to the *gold standard* which was in effect before the Depression.

Nations operating under the gold standard agreed to redeem their currency in gold when this was requested by any holder of that currency. While gold was not necessarily the means of exchange for world trade, it was the unit to which all currencies under the gold standard were pegged. Since all currencies in the system were linked to gold, exchange rates between those currencies were fixed.

Assume for the moment that there are no private purchases or sales of financial assets between citizens of different countries. Only goods and services are traded. Let's further assume that the United States and Great Britain are the only two countries which trade with each other. If Americans want to purchase British goods, they must convert their dollars into pounds. After all, British entrepreneurs want to be paid in pounds so that they can pay their workers. On the other hand, British citizens who want to buy American goods must convert their pounds into dollars. The rate at which pounds can be converted into dollars is called the *exchange rate*. Under the gold standard exchange rates were fixed because the values of currencies were linked to gold.

This fixed exchange rate system provided an adjustment mechanism that eliminated any excess supply or demand for currencies on the foreign exchange market at the fixed exchange rate. Suppose, for example, pounds are in excess supply on the foreign exchange market at the pegged exchange rate. The price level is too high in Britain. At the fixed exchange rate, British citizens desire to purchase "too many" American goods because they are cheap in comparison with British goods. Americans, however, purchase "too few" British goods because of their high price in comparison with American goods. To prevent a devaluation of the pound, the British government must be a residual buyer of pounds (seller of foreign currencies or gold). The increased supply of foreign currencies or gold and the increased demand for pounds (brought about by the purchases of pounds by the British government) will eliminate the excess supply of pounds on the foreign exchange market. The exchange rate will remain at its fixed level. However, the sale of foreign currencies or gold by the British government will reduce the stock of high-powered money in Great Britain just as would the sale of a bond in open market operations. The money supply in Great Britain will fall by a multiple of the contraction in the stock of high-powered money.

Consequently, under the fixed exchange rate rules, any country whose currency was in excess supply automatically experienced a reduction in their money supply. As explained in previous chapters, such a fall in the money supply will reduce total spending in that country, reducing the demand for imports as well as the demand for domestic output. As the demand for imports falls, British citizens will supply fewer pounds to the foreign exchange market. The fall in British prices resulting from the reduction in total spending will induce Americans to purchase more British goods at the fixed exchange rate, increasing the demand for pounds. Thus, the foreign exchange market will return to equilibrium with the supply and demand for pounds equal at the pegged exchange rate.

If pounds are in excess demand at the pegged exchange rate, the monetary authorities must be residual buyers of foreign currencies or gold and thus suppliers of pounds. Their aim is to prevent the pound from appreciating in terms of the dollar. In the process of buying foreign currencies, the stock of high-powered money in Great Britain will expand, creating a multiple expansion of the money supply. The resulting increase in British prices and income will increase the supply of pounds and reduce the demand for pounds at the fixed exchange rate, returning the foreign exchange market to equilibrium.

The essential feature of a truly fixed exchange rate system is that each country's monetary policy can no longer be controlled by the national central bank. The very act of purchasing or selling foreign exchange (currencies) to peg exchange rates produces a change in the money supply which returns the foreign exchange market to equilibrium. No country that submits to a truly fixed exchange rate discipline can have control over its money supply. The domestic price level must be determined by world prices. The domestic money supply reacts to purchases and sales of foreign exchange or gold to produce that price level.

During the 1930s central banks asserted their independence of the fixed exchange rate discipline. National central banks refused to allow an excess demand or supply of their currency in the foreign exchange markets to affect their own domestic money supplies. They were not going to give *balance of payments* problems priority over domestic economic considerations.

The impact of purchases or sales of foreign exchange on the stock of high-powered money can be offset through open market operations. A country forced to sell foreign exchange to support its currency's value can purchase bonds in open market operations to insulate the money supply from foreign exchange stabilization operations. These *sterilization policies* (the use of open market operations to offset the impact of purchases or sales of foreign exchange on the stock of high-powered money) will prevent the foreign exchange market from returning to equilibrium. If the money supply is unaffected, there will be no change in total domestic spending and prices to correct the balance of payments deficit. Excess demand for foreign exchange will persist. Eventually the country will run out of foreign exchange to sell in support of its own currency, resulting in the currency's devaluation. These currency crises are the outcome of differing monetary policies among nations. If central banks permit their money supplies to adjust in response to foreign exchange stabilization policies, no such crises need occur.

Truly fixed exchange rates can be maintained only if national monetary policies are coordinated so as to produce the same rate of inflation in all countries whose currencies are pegged to each other. If countries insist on pursuing independent monetary policies, exchange rates must eventually be realigned to reflect differences in purchasing power among currencies. Monetary policies that fail to reflect stabilization operations in the foreign exchange market are the cause of balance of payments problems.

In the 1930s practically all countries in the world were in a very serious depression. Central banks were unwilling to have their money supplies and aggregate demand contract just because of a balance of payments deficit. This effectively destroyed the automatic mechanism by which equilibrium is restored in the foreign exchange market. We could not, therefore, expect a truly permanently fixed exchange rate system to last forever. Virulent economic nationalism, born during the 1930s and surviving today, prevents most countries from allowing their money supplies to be dictated by the actions of people in other countries through the foreign exchange markets. Central banks today continue to be residual buyers and sellers of their own currency in times of balance of payments disequilibrium, but through their open market sales and purchases, they prevent changes in the money supply necessary to restore equilibrium. The mechanism which operated under the gold standard for bringing the foreign exchange market back into equilibrium has been effectively destroyed by sterilization operations.

While the world is no longer on a pure gold standard, fixed exchange rates have remained the rule among most nations. For some time now, though, Canada has had a *floating exchange rate*. Germany, too, has permitted its currency to float for various periods of time. Floating exchange rates permit the foreign exchange rate to return to equilibrium without any effect on the country's money supply. The exchange rate itself changes instead of the money supply. If countries do not peg exchange rates, supply and demand for currencies on the foreign exchange market will determine the exchange rate.

To illustrate the adjustment mechanism under a floating exchange rate system, let us return to our simplified world consisting of the U.S. and Great Britain. The demand for American goods by British citizens constitutes a supply of pounds to the foreign exchange market. The demand for pounds is derived from the demand for British goods by Americans. If prices in the United States rise by 10 percent while prices in Great Britain remain constant, the exchange rate must change to produce equilibrium in the foreign exchange market. If exchange rates remained constant, American goods would rise in price relative to British goods in both countries, pricing American goods out of the world market. The American inflation would reduce the supply of pounds to the foreign exchange market at the constant exchange rate because British citizens would buy fewer American goods at the increased price. The demand for pounds would increase at the fixed exchange rate because Americans would buy more British goods as the price of American goods increased relative to the price of British goods. When the exchange rate is allowed to adjust to the changes in supply and demand, however, the pound will appreciate by 10 percent in terms of the dollar. In the U.S., American goods will increase in price by 10 percent, but so will the dollar price of British goods, for it will take 10 percent more dollars to purchase each pound. In Great Britain, the price of British goods will remain constant, but so will the pound price of American goods, for it will take 10 percent fewer pounds to purchase each dollar.

If exchange rates are free to fluctuate in response to private supply and demand, each country can independently pursue its own monetary policy. Some countries may prefer high rates of monetary growth and inflation, while other countries maintain slower rates of monetary growth and price stability. Those countries with higher than average inflation rates will experience a devaluation of their currency relative to other currencies. No country's goods will be priced out of the world market through domestic inflation.

Germany has generally maintained a slower rate of monetary expansion and less inflation than have most countries of Western Europe and the United States. The German general wholesale price index was at the same level in 1969 as it was in 1964. During that same time period general wholesale prices in the United States, for example, increased by over 12 percent. As a result of these differing rates of inflation, Germany has continued to develop an export surplus. As world prices continued to rise at a faster rate than German prices, German goods became cheaper in comparison with non-German goods. German exports increased rapidly, but German imports were discouraged by the rapid increase in world prices at the fixed exchange rate. This trade surplus implies excess demand for Deutschemarks. In order to maintain the fixed exchange rate, the German government has had to purchase foreign exchange (mainly dollars) and sell Deutschemarks on the foreign exchange market. In November 1969 the German government finally stopped purchasing dollars and other foreign exchange. Immediately the Deutschemark appreciated in value and eventually the German government repegged its value at the new exchange rate. As inflation continued in the United States, the German government again had to purchase large inflows of dollars to prevent the Deutschemark from appreciating. Again in May 1971, the Germans stopped buying dollars and let the mark float up in value in comparison with the dollar. The recent history of the Deutschemark illustrates the difficulties of maintaining fixed exchange rates in the absence of coordinated monetary policies. If countries have different monetary policies resulting in different rates of inflation, exchange rates must eventually be realigned. The rash of currency crises the world has experienced in the last decade are the ultimate consequence of independent monetary policies in a world of fixed exchange rates.

The United States is in a rather special position under the rules of the International Monetary Fund. Under the current international monetary payments system, most countries in the world must peg their currencies to the dollar. Of course, there have been periods when Germany and Canada have let their currencies float rather than peg their exchange rates to dollars. Other countries have revalued or devalued their currencies in terms of the dollar by changing the exchange rate at which they peg their currency. The United States, though, is under no obligation to peg its currency in terms of other currencies. Until 1968 the United States had to peg the price of gold in terms of the dollar, but since that year even this obligation has been discontinued. Because of the special position of the dollar, it is not meaningful to discuss a floating dollar. Whether the dollar changes in value or not in terms of other currencies depends upon the actions of other countries, not the U.S. The U.S. does not peg the price of the dollar in terms of anything. Consequently, many economists refer to the current international monetary system as the "dollar standard."

# 25

# THE ECONOMICS
# OF THE DOLLAR STANDARD

The position of the dollar in the international monetary system has changed radically since the end of World War II. After World War II, free world representatives met in Breton Woods, New Hampshire to create a new international payments system to replace the gold standard. John Maynard Keynes was the head of the British delegation to that conference. At that time Great Britain was running a huge trade deficit. The pound would have to be devalued unless other countries continued to lend Britain foreign exchange to finance that trade deficit. In addition, Great Britain and the rest of Europe were devastated by the war and needed large amounts of imported capital to rebuild their productive capacity. If these countries had to reduce imports in order to eliminate the trade deficit, recovery from the war would be an agonizingly slow process. In view of Western Europe's situation, it is not surprising that John Maynard Keynes advocated a payments mechanism which would require surplus nations to finance the deficits of other nations by lending them foreign exchange. If surplus nations were forced to lend their foreign exchange to deficit nations indefinitely, fixed exchange rates could be maintained.

The American delegation, headed by Henry Dexter White, fought Keynes' proposal. The United States was a surplus nation which owned most of the world's gold stock. As a trade surplus nation the United States did not support Keynes' proposal, which would have forced the United States to lend foreign exchange to Europe. The American counter-proposal was finally adopted and the International Monetary Fund was created. The American plan called for fixed exchange rates and only limited obligations to lend to deficit nations. In the early postwar period, the United States did voluntarily lend large quantities of dollars to Europe under the Marshall Plan. These loans enabled European countries to finance their imports from the United States. Consequently, the problem Keynes feared concerning Europe's ability to finance the imports needed for recovery was solved by voluntary loans from the United States.

In the 1960s, however, the tables turned. The United States became a chronic deficit country in her balance of payments, although the balance of trade remained in surplus until 1971. Now the United States favored some arrangement obligating surplus nations to lend foreign exchange to deficit nations as in Keynes' proposal. The United States supported the creation of Special Drawing Rights (SDRs), which essentially enabled deficit nations to borrow from surplus nations. Although a modified proposal was adopted by the IMF in 1967, European nations were given a veto on the use of these SDRs. This, in effect, made the loans voluntary, rather than an obligation of the surplus countries. Paradoxically, the United States ended up advocating a proposal strongly resembling Keynes' original plan. This time the European nations balked and defeated it.

By 1960, the United States had started to lose gold. Under the IMF rules, the dollar was pegged to gold. The United States was obligated to redeem its currency in gold at $35 an ounce if requested to by a foreign holder of dollars. In effect the United States had to peg the price of gold. The balance of payments deficits of the United States resulted in large gold outflows by the early 1960s. Every Secretary of the Treasury during this period spent part of his tenure in office traveling to Europe to persuade foreign central banks to use their excess dollars to buy American financial securities instead of gold. In other words, we wanted those surplus nations to lend our dollars back. Quite a few countries went along with the American requests, particularly Germany. France did not.

De Gaulle continued to demand gold for dollars for two reasons. He thought that the loans to the United States would enable American companies to buy up industries in France in order to avoid the high tariff wall around the Common Market countries. He feared that French management could not compete with American know-how and that an Americanization of French industry would result. Probably the main reason, though, that he opposed financing the American deficit in the balance of payments by lending excess dollars back to the United States was that he felt some of these resources would be devoted to financing the Vietnam war, which he opposed.

De Gaulle continued purchasing gold from the United States until 1968. In that year the student-worker strike eliminated France's balance of payments surplus. The result of that strike was an inflation which put France at a competitive disadvantage in world trade. France no longer had the dollars with which to buy gold. One hot Sunday in August 1969, French President Pompidou was forced to devalue the franc by 14 percent.

Even before the student-worker strike in France, the United States took actions to insulate its gold stock from further losses. In March 1968 the United States took the bold step of announcing that it would no longer sell gold to private holders of dollars. A two-tier system of prices developed. Gold prices were unsupported in the private gold market, but the United States, theoretically, continued to sell gold to foreign central banks at $35 an ounce. However, since 1968, it has become evident that the United States will not allow balance of payments problems priority over domestic economic considerations. The United States has insulated its money supply from outside control by refusing to support the price of gold in the private gold market. Although the Treasury officially agrees to sell gold at $35 an ounce to foreign central banks, the monetary authorities in those countries realize the United States would refuse to honor that commitment in the face of an assault on our gold reserves. Since United States monetary policy has a tremendous impact on world trade, foreign countries must adjust to the United States' monetary policy.

Consider, for example, the countries whose rate of growth of nominal aggregate demand results in less inflation than the rate produced by the United States' monetary policy. If those countries do not attempt to peg exchange rates, their currencies will appreciate in terms of the dollar. The rate of appreciation of their currencies will offset the differences in the rates of inflation.

Alternatively, the central banks in those countries could purchase foreign exchange to prevent their currency from appreciating. If the purchase of foreign exchange is not offset by open market sales of financial securities by the central bank, the money supply will expand, increasing nominal spending. It is in this sense that some European countries accuse the United States of "exporting inflation." The rise in prices and income resulting from the monetary expansion will return the foreign exchange market to equilibrium by equalizing foreign rates of inflation with that of the United States.

Of course the monetary authority can prevent the money supply from expanding as a result of the purchase of foreign exchange by selling bonds in open market operations. These sterilization operations prevent the foreign exchange market from returning to equilibrium. The central bank would have to continue purchasing foreign exchange to prevent its exchange rate from appreciating. The sale of bonds in open market operations to sterilize the impact of foreign exchange operations on the money supply constitutes an involuntary loan of purchasing power to the United States.

Any time a country exports more than it imports, it acquires future claims to foreign goods. If a country voluntarily lends purchasing power to foreign individuals to finance the export surplus, there will be no excess supply of foreign exchange at the pegged exchange rate, for the purchase of foreign financial securities constitutes a demand for foreign exchange. This voluntary purchase of foreign financial securities enables foreign individuals to bid domestic output away from domestic purchase without creating inflation.

Consider the budget constraint of the private, nonbanking sector:

Changes in money balances = After-tax income
  − net purchases of financial securities issued by the domestic government sector or foreign individuals and governments
  − expenditures on goods and services

The gap between income and desired expenditures on goods and services necessary to permit an export surplus is created by the purchase of foreign financial securities. If individuals desire to maintain their money balances, they must reduce their desired expenditures on goods by an amount equal to the purchase of financial securities.

When the government finances the purchase of foreign exchange by selling bonds in open market operations, preventing an expansion of the money supply, the private sector (in the process of buying those government bonds) is indirectly lending purchasing power to the rest of the world. The purchase of government bonds creates the gap between income and private desired expenditures on goods necessary to finance the export surplus. The private sector is not, how-ever, voluntarily lending purchasing power to finance foreign expenditures on domestic output. If the private sector were willing to voluntarily lend purchasing power to the rest of the world, there would be no excess supply of foreign exchange. The fact that the government is forced to purchase foreign exchange (or foreign financial securities) and issue its own financial securities to finance the export surplus at the pegged exchange rate is evidence that the private sector would have preferred to use that purchasing power for do-mestic investment or consumption. Governments eventually will find it unpopular to finance the export surplus by granting loans to deficit countries at rates of return which are unattractive compared to domestic rates. These involuntary loans can be eliminated by allowing domestic inflation or currency revaluation to eliminate any excess supply of for-eign exchange.

What are the alternative policy choices facing a country whose monetary policy produces a higher rate of inflation than the United States? If the value of its currency is prevent-ed from depreciating in terms of the dollar, its currency will soon be in excess supply on the foreign exchange market. To peg the exchange rate, the government must sell foreign exchange or gold. This foreign exchange stabilization opera-tion will reduce the money supply, decreasing nominal spend-ing, unless the central bank makes an offsetting purchase of securities in its open market operations. The resulting fall in domestic prices and income will return the foreign exchange market to equilibrium.

The sterilization of foreign exchange operations by open market purchases of financial securities by the central bank prevents the money supply from falling, and the export deficit will persist. The open market purchase of financial securities by the government increases the purchasing power available to be spent on private domestic expenditures on goods. Since the money supply remains constant, individuals in the private sector can maintain their money balances and still spend more than their after-tax income only if foreign individuals or the government purchase financial securities from the private sector. Of course the government can peg the exchange rate only as long as it has foreign exchange reserves. Once those foreign exchange reserves are exhausted, the country must devalue its currency.

Many countries in the world are having a difficult time adjusting to the dollar standard. The recent inflation in the United States has considerably increased the United States' balance of payments deficit. In fact, for the first time in 20 years, the United States has a continuing trade deficit. Other countries are now deciding they no longer wish to involuntarily lend real resources to the United States. Germany solved the problem by allowing its mark to float in May 1971. Canada solved the problem by allowing its dollar to float. Holland did the same thing. Japan has felt the pressure even more. Japan's export prices have risen only 10 percent since 1963 while U.S. export prices have increased more than 20 percent. Consequently, there has been great pressure on the Japanese yen to revalue in terms of the dollar.

The Japanese have relaxed many of their restrictions on imports and the purchase of foreign financial securities in an effort to reduce their balance of payments surplus and also as a result of American threats of import restrictions. For instance, in 1971 they allowed their citizens to invest in the American stock market for the first time. Import quotas on more than 25 products were removed. Japan still has the option of revaluing the yen. By the time you read this book, the Japanese yen may cost more in terms of dollars, and a Ford may then be a better deal than a Toyota.

# 26
## THE ECONOMICS OF SAVING OUR BIG CITIES

A picture of 10 well-groomed men linking arms appeared in *Newsweek*'s edition of May 24, 1971, on page 74. The caption was "Grim Faces of 1971." Although the faces looked anything but grim, the sentiments of those men surely were. They were all mayors of big cities, part of a "mayors' lobby." Earlier in the year they and seven other big city mayors trooped en masse to D.C. What for? For money. For help. The big cities were in trouble (and most certainly still are). The mayors wanted the Congress to pass on the administration's *revenue-sharing* plan. Spread the federal tax revenues was the watchword. Before going into the specifics of revenue sharing, let's attempt to discover why the cities are in such bad shape.

We all know about the crime, pollution, health, and all other urban decay problems. But the quest for federal revenue sharing stems from the cities' steadily shrinking tax base. New York suffers from an exodus of corporations; New Orleans suffers from a similar exodus of middle-class homeowners who are heading for saner outlying parishes. More generally, though, the 1970s fiscal crisis in our nation's urban areas has been aggravated by the combined impact of recession and inflation on their taxing system, which consists mainly of sales and property taxes.

Whereas personal and corporate income taxes provide over 85 percent of total federal revenues, they only account for 16 percent of state and local tax revenues. The bulk of state and local revenues comes from property and sales taxes. When nominal income increases, federal income tax goes up even more than in proportion because of our progressive system. Property and sales tax revenues do not go up more than in proportion. Therefore they have been lagging behind federal income tax receipts. At the same time, expenditures at the public nonfederal level have skyrocketed.

Inflation has helped this, as have militant unions. From 1960 to 1971 the prices of the goods and services purchased by government increased almost 33 percent, which is fully 1.3 times as much as the consumer price index. Teachers and other public employees got wage increases equal to twice the national rate of growth. Since over 40 percent of all state and local expenditures are for wages, this fact is not insignificant in explaining at least part of the fiscal crisis.

Recession and inflation (at current rates) are really short-run problems and as such do not necessarily call for revenue sharing because the size of the aid would not necessarily get bigger during economic downturns. But the basic problem of property and sales taxes not growing fast enough to meet local needs is another story.

Granted that a fiscal crisis exists, how would revenue sharing work? General revenue sharing would involve a certain small percentage of total federal tax revenue being sent back to the states, no strings attached. The administration asked that the amount be equal to 1.3 percent of taxable personal income or about $5 billion in 1973. The transfer of funds would be automatic. States would then do what they thought best with the money.

General revenue sharing is of course not the only way to help out the states. If some form of universal, federally financed negative income tax or Family Assistance Plan is enacted, a great fiscal burden will be removed from the big cities. Fully $12.1 billion of state and local expenditures went to public welfare in 1969. Those states which offer the highest welfare checks have suffered the most because poor people have migrated to them in droves. If states and cities could rely on a uniform federal welfare program, this would no longer be a problem, and a large part of their current fiscal crisis would disappear.

The federal government could also engage in "tax sharing," returning a percentage of actual tax receipts to the state in which they were collected. No redistribution from rich states to poor states is possible with tax sharing, whereas it is with revenue sharing. (Whether or not it would actually work out that way is debatable, given the history of federal spending.)

States could either institute an income tax where it has not existed or raise the rates where it has. In fact, states could conceivably enact a progressive state income tax to avoid future fiscal crises.[1] States are individually very reluctant to do so, and for very good reason. If, say, Michigan taxes individual income progressively (or even proportionately) and no other states do, then, if other taxes remain the same, less people will move into Michigan, and some people may even move out. Other states will look better because of lower taxes. If Michigan taxes corporate income and no other states do, then fewer companies will establish themselves in Michigan and some may even move out. It is never to the advantage of a state to make the cost of working or being in business *relatively* higher than in other states. A federal income tax system is therefore preferred by the states because it applies equally throughout the country.

State and city officials vigorously defend revenue sharing out of nationally collected taxes because they feel that the taxing power of the federal government is greater than that

---

[1]However, in 1971 Pennsylvania's Supreme Court declared its progressive income tax unconstitutional.

of the individual states and cities. Just looking at the numbers, though, one would be hard pressed to agree with this idea. While it may be true for couples and string quartets, it cannot be true that in this case the sum of the parts is greater than the whole. The tax base of the federal government is exactly equal to all the state and local tax bases added together. However, the federal government has the power to pass tax laws which would perhaps never be passed by some individual state legislatures.

There may be an argument for economies of scale. Perhaps the centralization of all the tax data for all the country in massive computers in Washington, D.C. is cheaper than having each locality do its own assessing, filing, checking, and collecting. Administrative costs per unit of tax collected could be lower this way. But this technological argument does not imply support of *uniformity* of taxes for all locations. States and cities could still specify their chosen set of taxes.

Tax credits are another alternative to general revenue sharing which we have yet to discuss. Currently taxpayers can deduct from income the taxes they pay to the states and cities. Their federal tax burden is reduced by their marginal tax rate times the deduction. A tax credit would allow them to deduct all state and local taxes directly from their tax liabilities to the IRS. In this manner states would more easily be able to increase their taxes. No redistribution of revenue among states is possible with this scheme, however.

The federal government also exempts interest receipts from municipal bonds from federal income tax. This permits municipalities to borrow at lower interest rates. It is equivalent to a subsidy.

As another alternative to general revenue sharing, government officials have proposed what they call *special revenue sharing*. This program would essentially be a continuation of state grants-in-aid. Revenues would be given to the states for use in several major areas of social concern such as urban community development, education, rural community development, manpower training, law enforcement, and transportation. While laudable in intent, special revenue sharing would (or will) end up exactly like general revenue sharing. Suppose California gets special revenues earmarked for education, but it really wants to spend more on law enforcement. It need merely funnel state-raised tax dollars out of education (after it's used the federal funds there) and into law enforcement.

Many of you can do the same if you get earmarked money. Let's say your local credit union will only grant loans for "worthwhile" purposes. You want to buy a new 4-channel stereo for your car. You know the credit union won't consider that a worthwhile endeavor. So you go to the credit union and say you need money for school books. When you get the loan you may indeed spend it on school books, but you'll take the money you already had for school books and buy that quadraphonic tape deck for your car.

Politically, it is unrealistic to think that congressmen will support revenue sharing. Local politicians will get all the credit for the results of spending the shared revenue, while federal politicians will get all the blame for imposing the taxes which made the revenue sharing possible.

In any event, revenue sharing can't be free. When the federal government gives away some of its revenues, it faces a problem: if everything is to remain the same at the federal level, the U.S. government must run a deficit. If the Treasury is already running a deficit, it will run a larger one with revenue sharing. This increased deficit must be financed somehow: we discussed how in earlier chapters.

# 27
## THE ECONOMICS
## OF FUTURE PROSPERITY

As early as 1965, economists and politicians in the nation's capital declared that the United States economy had entered a new era in which traditional business cycle ups and downs in the economy were a thing of the past. Economists proclaimed that future endeavors on their part would merely involve "fine tuning." In November of 1968, the Bureau of the Census saw fit to change the title of its monthly publication *Business Cycle Development* to *Business Conditions Digest*. As late as November 1969, former Chairman of the Council of Economic Advisors Dr. Arthur M. Okun, was sanguine enough about the future of prosperity in the United States to write that "Today few research economists regard the business cycle as a particularly useful organizing framework for the overall analysis of current economic activity, and few teachers see 'business cycles' as an appropriate title for a course to be offered to their students." Okun went on to say that President Johnson's 1965 statement, "I do not believe recessions are inevitable," was no longer controversial. Okun felt that recessions were generally considered to be fundamentally preventable, "like airplane crashes, and unlike hurricanes."

Ironically, the National Bureau of Economic Research dates the start of the 1969-70 Recession in November of 1969. We then started on the twenty-seventh full-fledged slump in U.S. business history.

So the business cycle is back. We are still in a situation where there is relatively high unemployment and a high rate of inflation. Members of the administration continue to maintain that current policies are sufficient to bring about cuts in unemployment and inflation. Administration critics demand wage and price controls, job creation, a reinstatement of the investment tax credit, larger deficits, more accelerated depreciation, tax cuts, government restrictions on high interest rates, restrictions on foreign spending to improve our balance of payments deficit, and so on, ad nauseam. As quickly as critics describe what should be done, administration spokesmen describe what is being done and what has already been done. Every once in a while the Secretary of the Treasury is sent out to tell the American people that the government has provided "enormous" monetary and fiscal stimuli and that the "President very strongly feels that these things have been set in motion and that they must be permitted to have time to work."

How is the intelligent citizen to analyze the myriad details that are floating around concerning the present state of affairs in the United States? We feel that the preceding 26 chapters have presented readers of this book with a basic framework for analysis of national issues. It should be apparent by now that one critical aspect of any proposed policy involves the budget constraint. We are referring not only to the individual's budget constraint, but to the government's and to the world's. No person or government can continue expenditures without some means of financing them. A proposal for an investment tax credit must be linked with an explanation of how the reduction in government revenues due to the lower corporate taxes obtained will be made up as the government continues to maintain its expenditures. And if the government opts for bigger deficits, we must ask how the government will finance that deficit: by borrowing or by printing money?

It's hard to imagine that a mere 10 years ago Gunnar Myrdal felt compelled to tell the *Washington Post* that the world's greatest problem was "economic stagnation" in America. In that year, the United States started out on the longest period of uninterrupted expansion in its economic history. Although a new era had not begun, as was prophesized during that expansion and shattered by the 1969-70 Recession, the future of prosperity is nonetheless no different today than it was 10 years ago. The basic forces which drive our economy have not changed. The basic decisions facing consumers and entrepreneurs have not changed. The policy dilemmas facing administration officials have not changed. Hopefully, though, the reader's understanding of the economics of these national issues has changed.

On Sunday, August 15, shortly after this manuscript was sent to the publisher, President Nixon announced a radically new economic program to aid recovery from the 1969-70 Recession and to respond to the overvaluation of the dollar at the officially pegged exchange rate of several other countries. In one of the most dramatic political speeches on economic policy since Roosevelt's March 1933 New Deal speech, President Nixon proposed the following:

1. A freeze on wages, prices, and rents for 90 days.
2. Tax cuts totaling $6.3 billion in the current fiscal year:
   a. A repeal of the 7 percent excise tax on automobiles.
   b. Acceleration to January 1, 1972 of a $50 increase in personal income tax exemptions and an increase in the minimum standard deduction to 15 percent or a maximum of $2,000, both originally scheduled to occur the following year.
   c. A 10 percent investment tax credit on new, U.S.-built capital equipment retroactive to August 15, dropping to 5 percent on August 15, 1972.

3. A 10 percent surcharge on all dutiable imports.
4. Government spending cuts of $4.7 billion, resulting primarily from the temporary deferral of the revenue-sharing and welfare reform programs now before Congress and a 6-month freeze on a government pay increase planned for January 1.

In addition Nixon announced that the United States would no longer sell gold to foreign central banks at $35 an ounce, thus putting the world officially on a dollar standard. To the reader, most of the implications of the new Nixon economic program will be history. Because of the pertinence of Nixon's program to the issues discussed in this book, the authors cannot resist the opportunity to comment on Nixon's program before it becomes history.

First of all, Nixon's new economic program does not offer any significant test of the relative strengths of monetary and fiscal actions. If this program is carried out *intact*, it will provide little fiscal stimulus. The debate between the monetarists and the fiscal policy Keynesians centers on whether increases in the money supply or fiscal policy actions which raise the nominal rate of interest and thereby reduce the demand for money are the most effective means of stimulating aggregate nominal spending. The money supply during the first half of 1971 increased very rapidly, leading the monetarists to predict large increases in GNP for the next 6 months or more. The fiscal policy Keynesians were not as optimistic for they were concerned about the high rates of saving, partly in increased hoarded money balances, even in the face of an admittedly stimulating deficit. Most fiscal policy Keynesians, however, do not credit the Nixon economic program with providing much stimulus to the economy—if carried out *intact*. Dr. George Perry of the Brookings Institution, one of the leading fiscal policy Keynesians, quickly went on record predicting that the fiscal stimulus provided by the Nixon program was not big.

For a moment, consider the economic reasoning behind

this assessment of the fiscal policy effects of Nixon's economic program on aggregate nominal spending. The fiscal policy Keynesian argues that *pure fiscal actions*—government fiscal actions which do not affect the rate of monetary growth—increase the market rate of interest, inducing the public to hold fewer money balances relative to income. Rising nominal interest rates reduce the demand for money and stimulate total spending. In the context of that argument, assume that the Federal Reserve maintains a previously determined target rate of growth in the money supply through its open market operations. The tax cut will increase the after-tax income of the private sector. Some of this additional income might be spent on consumer goods, but typically most of it will be saved. The amount saved constitutes an increased supply of loanable funds. On the other hand, the investment tax credit increases profitable investment opportunities. The financing of these new investment opportunities will result in an increased demand for loanable funds at the current real rate of interest. In addition, if government spending were reduced by an amount less than the tax cut, the government would have to borrow more. In the Nixon program, however, proposed government spending cuts are actually slightly more than the tax cuts, implying that the government will be able to *reduce* its borrowing from the private sector. Tax cuts total $6.3 billion, but the increased tax receipts from the import surtax are expected to be $2.1 billion. Consequently, the net loss of revenue is only $4.2 billion. Since the cuts in government spending total $4.7 billion, the actual government deficit will be about $500 million less as a result of the whole program. The real rate of interest will tend to rise if at the former real rate of interest the savings out of the increased after-tax income is less than the increased funds needed to finance the new investment and automobile purchases minus the drop in government borrowing.

However, the net effect of these fiscal actions on the real rate of interest is probably less important in determining nominal interest rates (and therefore the cost of holding money) than are changes in inflationary expectations. Typically changes in the nominal rate of interest are not due to changes in the real rate of interest, but rather to changes in the expected rate of price change term. If Nixon's wage and price controls succeed in breaking the inflationary psychology, the expected rate of price change term may well be adjusted downward, causing a fall in nominal interest rates. In fact, this was the initial reaction of investors to the news of Nixon's program. The bond market rallied significantly (interest rates fell). Such decreases in the nominal interest rate would tend to increase the demand for money relative to income. Most monetarists however, would not expect either of these changes in the nominal rate of interest to have significant effect on the demand for money.

Although Nixon's new economic program is not designed to add significantly to nominal aggregate demand, it does change the structure of that spending through its use of taxes. The investment tax credit, the repeal of the automobile excise tax, and the import surcharge are all aimed at inducing consumers to spend more for some products and less on others. The increase in nominal aggregate demand resulting from stimulative monetary and fiscal policies has typically been concentrated in consumer durable industry, particularly housing. Nixon's new program is designed to increase spending in the producer durable and automobile sectors.

In 1971 forecasts of a 10-million-car year seemed wishful thinking as the year progressed and domestic sales were only running at an annual rate of 8 to 8.5 million. Foreign imports accounted for over 18 percent of new car sales. Fortunately for Detroit, the repeal of the automobile excise tax and the import surcharge will probably guarantee that 10-million-car year. The tariff on imports will increase from 3.5 percent to 10 percent, improving the price competitiveness of domestic as opposed to imported automobiles. The repeal of the excise tax on automobiles improves the price competitiveness of automobiles relative to other goods. Detroit can use that 10-million-car year because unemployment rates in the city of Detroit have reached 14 percent.

The stock market reacted to Nixon's program, producing a large appreciation in the value of domestic automobile stocks. The owners of American Motors experienced a 30 percent appreciation in the value of their stock virtually overnight. By contrast, the Japanese appear to be the big losers because of the import surcharge. The price of Sony stock dropped 3 points the day after Nixon's announcement.

Because of general excess capacity and previous repeal of the investment tax credit, the producer durable sector—principally the machine tool and computer industries—had experienced a drastic drop in sales. The reinstatement of the investment tax credit will stimulate spending in these sectors. Moreover, domestic producer durables will have an over-whelming competitive advantage over foreign imports be-cause of the 10 percent import surcharge plus the fact that the investment tax credit does not apply to purchases of imported producer durables.

If the net increase in loanable funds resulting from the tax cut and the simultaneous cut in government spending is not sufficient to finance the new investment and the new install-ment credit needed for new car purchases, real rates of interest will rise. In that case funds probably will be bid away from mortgage lenders, reducing effective demand for resi-dential housing. It is not certain that real interest rates must rise, however, if government spending is reduced as much as desired by the President.

The Nixon administration was previously concerned with increasing the total level of nominal aggregate demand. With the new economic policy the emphasis has shifted to an attempt to direct this increased demand into specific sectors of the economy. Eventually, following such a policy of stabilization of *sectoral* demands (rather than limiting govern-ment activity to the stabilization of *total* aggregate demand) may threaten consumer sovereignty. Bottlenecks and structural unemployment may be the symptoms of a transitional phase needed to effect the transfer of productive resources from one sector to another in response to changes in consumer tastes. If stabilization goals include the use of excise taxes and tariffs to divert demand away from bottlenecks into industries with deficient demand for labor, consumer sovereignty could be impaired. Changes in excise taxes could be used to offset consumer preferences, eliminating the discomfort (the economic cost) of shifting resources from one sector to another. Consumer preferences would cease to allocate resources. Resources would be allocated to satisfy government stabilization objectives. Consumer tastes would simply allocate taxes.

The import surtax is a response to the overvaluation of the dollar at the officially pegged exchange rates of several other countries—especially Japan. (The German mark has floated up in value about 10 percent since May.) This overvaluation of the dollar has tended to give imports in the U.S. a competitive advantage in several industries, notably steel, automobiles, and textiles. Remember, though, that imports are financed by the purchase of American exports or by an increase in credit extended the United States by foreign countries. If the U.S. money supply is held constant, increased imports have little effect on *total* aggregate demand for American goods. They merely shift demand away from import-competing goods to exports and goods purchased with foreign credit. As long as the money supply is not affected, trade deficits need not reduce total effective demand for American goods.

The import duties may improve the United States' position in negotiations for tariff reductions. Hopefully the import surcharge will be traded for reductions in foreign barriers to American goods and agreements to increase the flexibility of exchange rates.

Until this summer, the Nixon economic game plan relied

on an increase in aggregate nominal demand to stimulate employment and output. The rapid rise in GNP during the first half of 1971 consisted mainly of price increases, not increases in output. The inflationary expectations generated by 4 years of accelerating inflation continued to sustain high rates of inflation in the face of high unemployment. Workers, expecting future inflation, raised their wage demands to protect their future purchasing power despite high rates of unemployment. Producers, in turn, passed the increased labor costs on to consumers in higher prices. Higher prices, though, reduce demand for final output, reducing the demand for labor. Consequently, rising labor costs prevented the rapid increases in GNP that occurred during the first half of 1971 from occurring as increases in output. Most of the increase in total spending occurred as inflation as producers passed high labor costs on in higher prices.

Nixon's solution to this problem is a wage and price freeze. All wages, prices, and rents will be frozen for 90 days. If effectively enforced, this freeze will eliminate changes in the official price indexes during that 90-day period. If prices cannot rise in response to increased nominal aggregate demand, consumers will demand more final output. The Nixon administration hopes that this increase in demand for final output can be satisfied by increased employment of labor. Producers will have an incentive to hire more labor and increase their output. Even though wages and prices are frozen, profits are not. Producers can increase profits, even though profit margins are fixed, by increasing sales of final output. If producers succeed in hiring additional labor at the controlled wage rates during the wage and price freeze, no shortages need develop.

The supply of labor forthcoming under the wage and price freeze will decide its success. Nixon hopes that unemployed workers will supply sufficient labor services at the controlled wage rates to supply enough output to prevent shortages at the controlled price level. Of course, if wage and price controls continue for a substantial period of time in the face of increasing nominal aggregate demand, shortages will occur. Eventually producers will find it difficult to hire labor at the controlled wage rates. If output cannot increase rapidly enough to satisfy consumer demand at the controlled price level, shortages will develop. No severe shortages are likely to develop in 90 days. For longer periods of time, though, effectively enforced wage and price controls would certainly create widespread shortages or black markets if aggregate nominal demand continued to increase at rapid rates.

INDEX

# INDEX

176